Language checkpoints

Written by JACK NORMAN &
MARK FLETCHER
Illustrated by GRAHAM WALL

Language checkpoints

Written by *JACK NORMAN* &
MARK FLETCHER
Illustrated by *GRAHAM WALL*

M

Acknowledgements

While every care has been taken to trace and acknowledge copyright, the publishers tender their apologies for any accidental infringement where copyright has proved untraceable. They would be pleased to come to a suitable arrangement with the rightful owner in each case.

Angus and Robertson Publishers for the extract from *Pigs Might Fly* by Emily Rodda, (c) Emily Rodda, 1986; Colin Thiele and Rigby Publishers for the excerpt from *The Sknuks*.

Copyright © Mark Fletcher and Jack Norman 1989
Illustrations copyright © The Macmillan Company of Australia 1989
Cover design and illustration by Graham Wall

All rights reserved
No part of this publication
may be reproduced or transmitted
in any form or by any means
without permission

First published 1989 by
THE MACMILLAN COMPANY OF AUSTRALIA PTY LTD
107 Moray Street, South Melbourne 3205

6 Clarke Street, Crows Nest 2065
Reprinted 1990

Associated companies and representatives
throughout the world

National Library of Australia
cataloguing in publication data

Fletcher, Mark.
    Language checkpoints 1.

    ISBN 0 333 50049 0.

    1. English language — Juvenile literature.   I. Norman, Jack.   II. Wall, Graham, 1938–   III. Title.

428

Set in Palatino by Setrite Typesetters Ltd, Hong Kong
Printed in Hong Kong

Contents

Unit 1   FOCUS   Narrative: The Sknuks   7
            CHECKPOINT 1   Discussion time   10
            CHECKPOINT 2   Exploring words   11
            CHECKPOINT 3   Building blocks   13
            CHECKPOINT 4   Action time   15
            CHECKPOINT 5   Moving on   17

Unit 2   FOCUS   Instructions: Making a glove puppet   19
            CHECKPOINT 1   Discussion time   21
            CHECKPOINT 2   Exploring words   22
            CHECKPOINT 3   Building blocks   24
            CHECKPOINT 4   Action time   26
            CHECKPOINT 5   Moving on   29

Unit 3   FOCUS   Verse: The Teams   30
                           Interstate Driver   32
            CHECKPOINT 1   Discussion time   33
            CHECKPOINT 2   Exploring words   34
            CHECKPOINT 3   Building blocks   36
            CHECKPOINT 4   Action time   39
            CHECKPOINT 5   Moving on   42

Unit 4   FOCUS   Recipes: Recipe 1 — Chocolate fudge   43
                           Recipe 2 — Fairy cakes   45
                           Recipe 3 — Chocolate-chip cookies   46
            CHECKPOINT 1   Discussion time   47
            CHECKPOINT 2   Exploring words   49
            CHECKPOINT 3   Building blocks   51
            CHECKPOINT 4   Action time   53
            CHECKPOINT 5   Moving on   55

Unit 5   FOCUS   News report: A long road for Lloyd and
                           an L-plate pup   57
            CHECKPOINT 1   Discussion time   59
            CHECKPOINT 2   Exploring words   60
            CHECKPOINT 3   Building blocks   62
            CHECKPOINT 4   Action time   64
            CHECKPOINT 5   Moving on   65

Unit 6   FOCUS   Narrative: Pigs Might Fly   66
            CHECKPOINT 1   Discussion time   69
            CHECKPOINT 2   Exploring words   70
            CHECKPOINT 3   Building blocks   72
            CHECKPOINT 4   Action time   74
            CHECKPOINT 5   Moving on   76

Unit 7   FOCUS   Diaries, logs and journals:
                        Robinson Crusoe   78
                        Bidu's journal   80
            CHECKPOINT 1   Discussion time   81
            CHECKPOINT 2   Exploring words   82
            CHECKPOINT 3   Building blocks   84
            CHECKPOINT 4   Action time   86
            CHECKPOINT 5   Moving on   88

Unit 8   FOCUS   Advertisements: Cuddly Cat   89
                        Jay's Joggers   90
            CHECKPOINT 1   Discussion time   91
            CHECKPOINT 2   Exploring words   92
            CHECKPOINT 3   Building blocks   94
            CHECKPOINT 4   Action time   96
            CHECKPOINT 5   Moving on   97

Unit 9   FOCUS   Article: The feathertail glider   100
            CHECKPOINT 1   Discussion time   102
            CHECKPOINT 2   Exploring words   104
            CHECKPOINT 3   Building blocks   106
            CHECKPOINT 4   Action time   108
            CHECKPOINT 5   Moving on   110

Unit 10   FOCUS   Letters: From Jane to Alison   111
                        The fuel pump complains   112
            CHECKPOINT 1   Discussion time   113
            CHECKPOINT 2   Exploring words   114
            CHECKPOINT 3   Building blocks   116
            CHECKPOINT 4   Action time   118
            CHECKPOINT 5   Moving on   122

UNIT 1
FOCUS   Narrative

This extract was taken from a book by Colin Thiele called *The Sknuks*. It is a simple allegory for children that teaches one of the fundamental truths of our time: that we are destroying our own habitat and endangering our own survival.

The Sknuks
Colin Thiele

Once upon a planet there were some creatures called Sknuks. They had legs and arms and ears, and an opening in the front of their heads.

The planet where the Sknuks lived was called Htrae. It was the loveliest planet of all, like a speck of gold in the sky. There were golden fields of wheat, and fruit trees with golden fruit, and gardens with golden flowers.

There were forests of tall trees, and beautiful blue mountains, and rivers of sparkling water and seas like a million mirrors. And there was green grass and bright sand and warm sunshine. The Sknuks were very lucky.

There were other creatures on Htrae as well as the Sknuks. There were birds with feathers as soft as down and as bright as rainbows. They sang in the mornings and they sang in the evenings and they sang all day long, until the land overflowed with their singing.

The Sknuks should have been happy with companions like that.

And there were tigers with coats of velvet and panthers with eyes like jewels. There were horses and whippets and antelopes that could arch and leap and run surer and swifter than sunlight. And there were eagles like gods in the sky.

There were salmon in the rivers that bent their backs like boomerangs and flung themselves higher than waterfalls. There were undersea gardens of coral filled with fish that were arrows of fire. There were whales like moving islands, and tuna like steel-blue bullets, and porpoises tumbling with fun.

The Sknuks should have been happy to share Htrae with creatures like that.

There were butterflies with wings of gold dust that were finer than the blue evening mist; orchestras of insects that played in the fields and forests; lizards with tongues that were darker than night-time and with scales like plates of rock; even worms that spun silk for the clothing of kings and queens.

There were diamonds on the planet of Htrae. There were rubies like drops of wine, and sapphires like chips of the sea, and opals like flames of fire. And there was gold underground in nuggets that were bigger than melons, and silver that gleamed when it melted, like beads of morning frost, and copper that ran from the cauldrons in rivers of shining sunlight. And there were caverns of coal as big as cathedrals and hidden lakes of oil and monstrous mountains of iron.

Beautiful, beautiful planet of Htrae! The Sknuks should have been singing a happy song about it:
  'Every day
  In every way
  It's good to be living
  In a place like Htrae.
  We're lucky, we're lucky
  At every pitch
  To be living on a planet
  So rare and rich.'

But the Sknuks were not happy.

They growled and grumbled, and pillaged and plundered, and squabbled and squandered. They eyed and they envied, grew frantic and frenzied, they coveted and craved and threatened and raved. They even stole from their neighbours and spied on their friends.

FOR THEY WERE GREEDY.

CHECKPOINT 1
Discussion time

Comment and answer
1. Why do you think the author called the planet where the Sknuks lived, Htrae?
2. In what ways was the planet of Htrae similar to our planet Earth?
3. What is your opinion of the way the Sknuks behaved towards each other?
4. The author says that the Sknuks should have been happy on the planet of Htrae. Why do you think they should have been happy?
5. What has been written to make you think that the planet of Htrae was a beautiful place?
6. What other creatures lived on the planet of Htrae along with the Sknuks?
7. What do you think caused the Sknuks to grumble and squabble?
8. What do you think will be the result of all the growling and stealing?
9. How do you think you would have felt if you had lived on the planet Htrae with the Sknuks?
10. Predict what you think will happen to the Sknuks and their planet of Htrae.
11. Look at these statements and decide if you think they are true or false. Make sure that you have a reason for your decision.
    a) The Sknuks were unhappy because they were jealous of each other.
    b) The planet of Htrae was spoilt by the birds, animals and forest creatures of the planet.
    c) The planet of Htrae was a very drab place with little colour and no natural beauty.
    d) Our planet Earth was like the planet Htrae before humans spoilt much of the environment.
    e) Htrae was a beautiful planet with tall forests, blue mountains and bright warm sunshine.

CHECKPOINT 2
Exploring words

Missing words

1. Here is a passage about the Sknuks with some of the words left out. Complete the passage using the most suitable word from the words given below. There may be more than one word that will fit but choose the word you consider the most suitable.

   The Sknuks lived on one of the most beautiful (1) in the universe. There was (2) the Sknuks could ever wish (3). It was a place of sparkling (4), (5) grass and (6) flowers. The Sknuks (7) have been very happy but they (8). They (9) and (10) and were very unhappy.

   1. planets, spheres, globes
   2. nothing, everything, something
   3. to, of, for
   4. clouds, water, sand
   5. blue, brown, green
   6. colourful, drab, grey
   7. could, should, might
   8. weren't, were, are
   9. laughed, grumbled, snarled
   10. fought, squabbled, quarreled.

Singular and plural

> A naming word that talks about only one thing is said to be *singular*. A naming word that talks about two or more things is said to be *plural*.
>
> | | Singular | | Plural |
> |---|---|---|---|
> | | dog + (s) | | dogs |
> | | cat + (s) | | cats |

1. What is the plural of these words?
   a) boy
   b) cow
   c) kitten
   d) girl
   e) hat

Prefixes

Read this sentence.

The Sknuks should have been *happy* but they were *unhappy*.

happy — unhappy

The meaning of the word 'happy' has been changed by using the *prefix* 'un'.

1. Change the meanings of these words using the prefix 'un'.
   a) do — undo
   b) wind — unwind
   c) plug — unplug
   d) fit — unfit
   e) healthy — unhealthy

2. Can you find other words that use the prefix 'un'?

unhappy   unload   unlike   undressed   unclean

8.3.91

CHECKPOINT 3
Building blocks

Nouns — naming words

In the story about the Sknuks many of the names used were made from the jumbled letters of naming words we use.

The planet *Htrae* is *Earth*.
The word for a father Sknuk was a *nam*, which is really a *man*.
The word for a mother Sknuk was a *namow*, which is really a *woman*.
The name for a little Sknuk was a *dik*, which is really a *kid*.
The name given to the grey paste that was spread all over the ground was *tnemec*, which is really *cement*.

We call naming words or words that name things *nouns*.

1. Unjumble these naming words to find the noun used in these sentences. *Fish*
    a) The *hisf* were swimming in the sea.
    b) The children were playing in the *rapk*. *Park*
    c) The *leppoe* lived on a planet called Earth. *People*
2. Make up three sentences using nouns with jumbled letters.

Complete the sentence
1. These are not complete sentences. Something is missing. Can you suggest how to make them complete sentences?
    a) Down the street *I saw a Rabbit*.
    b) 'Not now,' *the old man said* the young lad.
    c) *I climbed* over the fence.
    d) During the vacation we *went* to the zoo.
2. Compare the parts you supplied to complete the sentences with the parts supplied by other class members. Discuss the different ways the sentences were completed.

8.3.91

Cartoon capers

Read and enjoy this cartoon strip.

The conversation bubbles contain the exact words spoken by the cartoon characters.

1. Look at this cartoon strip. The conversation bubbles have been left empty. Can you suggest words to fill the conversation bubbles. Write down the exact words that you have chosen.

.8.3.91.

CHECKPOINT 4
Action time

Similes

Look at this sentence from our focus story.

There are birds with feathers *as soft as down* and *as bright as rainbows*.

The *italicised* phrases are a figure of speech known as a *simile*. In a simile, two things are compared. In one of the similes above, the colour of the birds' feathers is compared with the colours of the rainbow. Similes begin with the words 'like' or 'as'. We use similes in our writing and speech to create pictures with words.

1. Can you find other examples of similes in the story about the Sknuks?
2. Supply the missing words in these common similes.
   a) As _____ as a fox
   b) As cold as _____
   c) As dry as a _____
   d) As shy as a _____
   e) As _____ as soot
3. Think of some comparisons to complete these sentences and underline the simile.
   a) The cloud floated above us like <u>a ballon</u>.
   b) The jewels sparkled like <u>sun shine</u>.
   c) The old man looked fierce but turned out to be as gentle <u>as a cat</u>.
   d) The colours flashed in the sun like <u>gold</u>.
   e) His sharp pointed nose was like <u>a knife</u>.

15

What do you think?
1. The Sknuks were very stupid and spoilt their planet with their greed and by not caring for their environment. If they had the chance to start all over again what do you think they would do? Write a paragraph telling what you think they should do about:
   - the rivers and streams
   - the forests
   - the creatures
   - the buildings
   - the air or atmosphere.

   You may wish to use such words as:

   > conserve   environment   habitat
   > pollution   overcrowding   protect

Finish the story
1. Here is a story for you to finish. Don't forget to give your story a name or title.

   > The children, Grant and Melissa, had never seen such a beautiful spot. The trees stood straight and tall like soldiers and the birds and butterflies flittered from bush to bush and the air was filled with the sweet smell of recent rain.
   >
   > They decided that this ...

CHECKPOINT 5
Moving on

Task 1 Write to a friend
Pretend that you lived among the Sknuks. Write to a friend telling them about all the things that the Sknuks did to destroy their beautiful planet of Htrae.

Task 2 Just pretend
Imagine that people from space visited the Sknuks and tried to help them. The space people said that they would return in fifty years to see what had happened. Pretend that you return to Earth in fifty years time. What do you think you would see?

17

Task 3 Decode the message

Decode this special message from the space people to the Sknuks.

Here is the code:

A	B	C	D	E	F	G	H	I	J	K
4	6	5	8	1	15	3	22	9	11	13
L	M	N	O	P	Q	R	S	T	U	V
18	7	16	2	20	17	23	10	24	12	25
W	X	Y	Z							
19	21	14	26							

Here is the message:

__ __ / __ __ __ / __ __ __ __ /
8 2   16 2 24   7 4 13 1

__ __ __ __ .
19 4 23 10

__ __ __ __ __ __ / __ __ __ /
18 9 10 24 1 16   4 16 8

__ __ __ __ __ / __ __ __ __ .
18 1 4 23 16   19 1 18 18

UNIT 2
FOCUS   Instructions

Follow these instructions to make this neat glove puppet.

Make a glove puppet

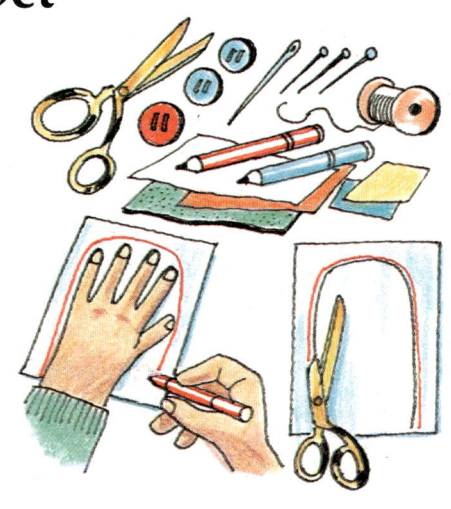

1. Collect these items: scissors, sewing needles, pins, embroidery cotton, pieces of felt or material, three buttons (two the same for the eyes and one bigger for the nose) felt pens, sheets of paper.
2. Place your hand on a piece of paper and draw round it with a pencil.
3. Cut out the shape you have drawn. This is the pattern for your puppet.

4. Pin the pattern onto the felt or material and then cut round it.
5. Repeat instruction 4 so that you have two pieces the same shape and size.
6. Decide where you want the eyes and the nose and sew on the buttons.
7. Use felt pens to draw the mouth.
8. Place the two pieces one on top of the other exactly with the 'face' in towards the other piece.
9. Sew along all the edges except the straight edge.
10. Turn the puppet inside out and it is ready for use.

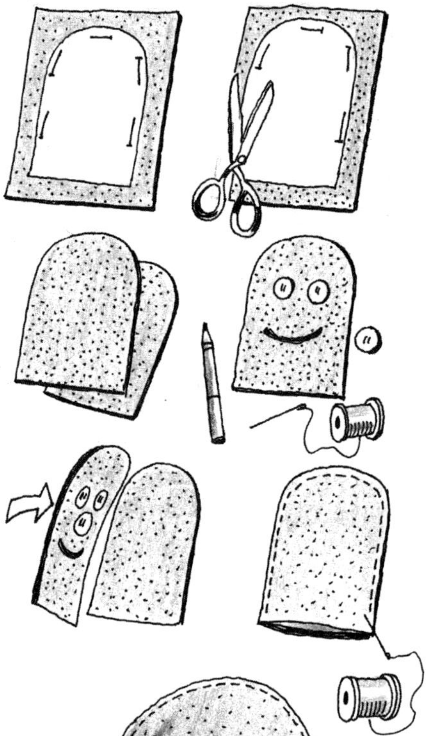

If you wish, you can decorate your puppet with other scraps of materials and buttons.

CHECKPOINT 1
Discussion time

Comment and answer
1. Arrange these instructions in the correct time sequence.
   a) Cutting out the pattern
   b) Sewing on the buttons
   c) Drawing round your hand with a pencil
   d) Turning the puppet inside out
   e) Sewing along all the edges
2. Are these statements true or false?
   a) The pattern allows you to use either hand in the puppet.
   b) It would be possible to have arms on the puppet if the pattern was changed.
   c) It would be possible to form the mouth in another way than simply drawing it on.
3. How would you change the pattern if you wanted to make a clown puppet?
4. Why do you think instruction 8 said to place 'the face in towards the other piece'?
5. What would have happened if the pattern had been made smaller than your hand?
6. What would be the result if you sewed all the edges, including the straight edges?

CHECKPOINT 2
Exploring words

Word opposites — antonyms

> Words which are opposite in meaning are called *antonyms*. These words are antonyms:
>
>   **same — different   bigger — smaller**
>   **neat — untidy**

1. Can you write the antonyms of these words?
   - a) top
   - b) downwards
   - c) straight
   - d) inside
   - e) under
   - f) find
   - g) fact
   - h) even
   - i) buy

Double words — compound words

> Two words joined together can make a new word.
>
>   **hand + some = handsome**
>   **in + side = inside**
>   **an + other = another**
>
> These words can be called *compound* words.

1. Add the first word to the second. What are the new compound words?
   - a) skate + board = _____
   - b) down + hill = _____
   - c) sand + paper = _____

2. Match the words in the cloud on left with words in the cloud on the right to make compound words. Use these compound words in the sentences at the top of the next page.

    week   news   out   end   side   paper
    any   down how   thing ever stairs

a) She collected the _____ from the front gate.
b) They did not see _____ in the large bag.
c) They were to go to the farm at the _____.
d) _____ the house she played on the lawn.
e) All the children went _____.
f) '_____ many you catch I will buy them all,' the collector answered.

Build-a-word

Look over these three words.

make   shape   face

The word stems 'ake', 'ape', and 'ace' were used.

1. Add these beginning letters to the word stem 'ake'.
    r,   fl,   sn,   br,   st,   qu,   sh
2. Add these beginning letters to the word stem 'ape'.
    g,   t,   dr,   scr,   gr,   esc
3. Now add these beginning letters to this word stem 'ace'.
    l,   p,   pl,   gr,   tr,   sp

Word families

Let us build up some word families.
Here's one.

flake   flakes   flaked   flaking

1. Build word families for these words
    a) stake   d) place
    b) scrape   e) trace
    c) escape

CHECKPOINT 3
Building blocks

Verbs — action words

> Look over the instructions in the focus. The first word in each is a special word. They are action words. They tell what has to be done.
>
> **Collect** ...
> **Place** ...
> **Cut** ...
> **Pin** ...
> **Decide** ...
>
> Each sentence has the same form.
>
> Action or instruction word → *Cut* **out the shape.**
> → *Pin* **the balloon onto the felt.** ← What has to be done
> → *Use* **felt pens to draw the mouth.**

1. Look over these instructions. Which are the action or instruction words?
    a) Add the two numbers together.
    b) Buy several bottles of milk.
    c) Select one of these books.
    d) Read all the information on the page.
    e) Return the box to the shed.
2. Add suitable action words to these instructions.
    a) _____ the paper on the table.
    b) _____ the apples from the tree.
    c) _____ the clip onto the puppet.
    d) _____ the dishes for me.
    e) _____ all the surface of the car.
    f) _____ the body of the dead animal.

24

Capitals and full stops

Notice in each instruction there is a capital letter for the first action word. There is also a full stop at the end of the instruction.

Capital letter → **Cut out the shape you have drawn.** ← Full stop

All sentences, whether instructions or not, need a capital letter at the beginning and a full stop at the end.

1. Look over these instructions. Where are capital letters and full stops needed?
   a) take the pencil to the table
   b) unlock the double gate
   c) tie the horse up to the hitching rail
   d) open the door of the garage
   e) wash down the dirty windows

2. All types of sentences need a capital letter to begin and a full stop at the end. Try giving these sentences full stops and capital letters.
   a) last week I saw Lisa at the show
   b) he has been to Melbourne many times
   c) fix the clock for me please
   d) the rust looks very dangerous
   e) buy as many of those shrubs as you can

CHECKPOINT 4
Action time

Observe and write

1. The pictures in the sequence below show how to make a monster puppet. Study each picture carefully. Write the instructions or directions that could be used with each picture. After you have finished writing the instructions you may wish to make the monster puppet.

   Items needed:

   one egg carton   a woollen sleeve   two white
                          from an adult's   cardboard circles
                          old cardigan   and two smaller
                                                   red cardboard
                                                   circles

   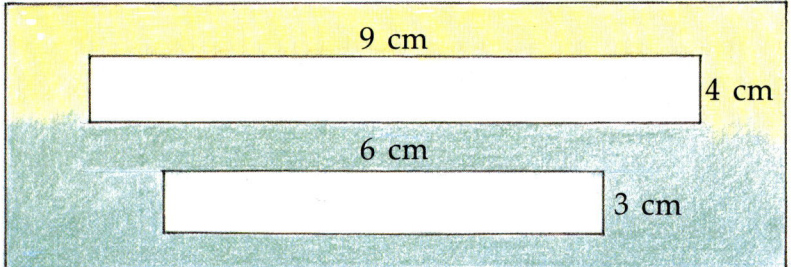

   two cardboard strips

26

What to do:

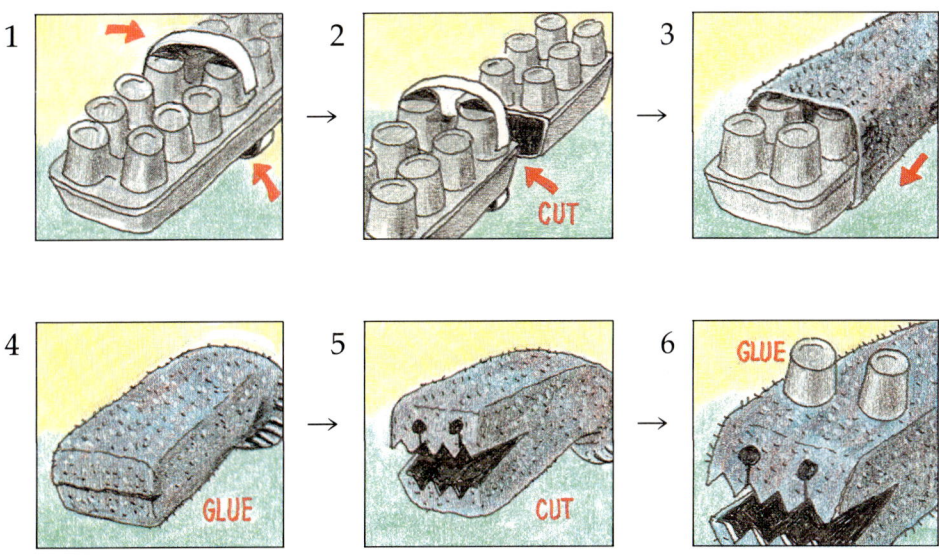

Read and rewrite

1. Below are some directions on how to make a balloon rocket. Read the instructions carefully. Study the illustrations as well. Then rewrite the directions in your own words. Write them in order, one under the other and number them 1, 2, 3, ...

   You will need:
   - a thin piece of cardboard large enough to be wrapped around a milk bottle
   - four aluminium tins about 12 centimetres in length
   - a long balloon
   - a circular piece of cardboard with a 1 centimetre hole in the centre

   What to do:
   The first thing to do is to wrap the piece of cardboard around the milk bottle and glue it firmly. Then the tins can be glued onto the cardboard and the circular piece of cardboard onto the base. When the glue has set you can slide the cylinder off the bottle. It is now ready for you to put the balloon inside. Make sure that the nozzle of the balloon hangs out below the cylinder. Now you are ready to launch the rocket. Blow the balloon up until the rounded end appears at the top of the cylinder. Hold the balloon rocket in the air. When you let the nozzle of the balloon go, the rocket will fly into the air.

Write some directions

1. Many different kinds of games are played in the playground. These games have many different rules. Some of them do not have rules that are written down. Choose a school game and prepare a set of rules for it. Don't try any of the major games like football, netball or cricket.

CHECKPOINT 5
Moving on

Task 1 Put on a puppet play
To prepare for this play you would need to make four puppets. The four puppets would be a little girl, a wolf, an old lady and a woodcutter. What would be the name of the puppet play? You could use sock puppets quite easily with the faces drawn on them. Discuss the dialogue, or what each puppet will say, and the actions before you start.

Task 2 Make a collection
Make a collection of instructions; recipes, directions which tell how to assemble some item of furniture or toy or how to use a kitchen or household appliance, or directions for games. Imagine you had to prepare instructions telling how to use something in your classroom. Jot down these directions. Discuss them with other classmates.

Task 3 Sketch and plan
The 'telework' is an imaginary invention. It is a television set that completes your homework while you watch your favourite shows. Prepare sketches and plans of this great invention. Then prepare a set of instructions for others who would want to use this machine.

UNIT 3
FOCUS　　　　　　　Verse

Read these poems. The first, 'The Teams', is about a form of transport that was used in the past. The second, 'Interstate Driver', is about a much newer form of transport.

The Teams

A cloud of dust on the long white road,
   And the teams go creeping on
Inch by inch with the weary load;
And by the power of the green-hide goad
   The distant goal is won.

With eyes half-shut to the blinding dust,
   And necks to the yokes bent low,
The beasts are pulling as bullocks must;
And the shining tires might almost rust
   While the spokes are turning slow.

With face half-hid 'neath a broad-brimmed hat
   That shades from the heat's white waves,
And shouldered whip with its green-hide plait,
The driver plods with a gait like that
   Of his weary, patient slaves.

Henry Lawson

Interstate Driver

The river is a wide band of pale reflected light,
as the ironbark of the bridge swish-swishes
past us like the ghosts of rushing silk-skirted women.

Then on we drive towards the pale sky of the east;
with one star shining above a wall of mist.

The next town is a few lights blinking,
a puff of steam from a shunting engine,
one black-coated fireman crossing the broad road.

Then out past the last thin cluster of trees;
the cushioned thunder of our tyres enters the sleeping desert.

Suddenly the oncoming semi-trailer
winks its headlights, winks again;
we realize that the stars are gone;
it is time the dawn switched off our lights
as we race on through the tingling air.

Ian Mudie

CHECKPOINT 1
Discussion time

Comment and answer
1. Which form of transport is the theme for 'The Teams'?
2. Why has the poet used the phrase 'inch by inch'?
3. Why has the poet used the phrase 'the shining tires might almost rust'?
4. What do you think would happen to the bullock teams in very wet weather?
5. In what ways do you think bullock-team transport is different from today's methods of transportation?
6. Which form of transport is the theme for 'Interstate Driver'?
7. Are there any other forms of transport mentioned in 'Interstate Driver'?
8. What are some problems and dangers faced by interstate drivers?
9. Compare the problems and dangers faced by an interstate driver with those faced by the bullock-team driver. Are there any the same? What are the differences?
10. Read over the outline sentence stems for 'Interstate Driver'. Can you complete these sentences?
    a) The truck passes _____
    b) Towards the _____
    c) A black-coated fireman _____
    d) The truck moves on _____
    e) An oncoming truck _____
    f) We switch _____

CHECKPOINT 2
Exploring words

'Same sound' words — homophones

> Some words have the same sound but different meanings.
>
> > by — buy   won — one
> > gate — gait   mist — missed
>
> These words are called *homophones*.

1. Write the homophones of these words and then use the words and their homophones in sentences.
   a) see   d) through   g) whether   j) plane
   b) current   e) there   h) flour   k) fought
   c) herd   f) warn   i) sore

Words with apostrophes — contractions

> Look over this sentence.
>
>
>
> **'It's** not in the large box,' she answered.
>
> 'It's' is the short form of 'it is'. Shortened words such as 'it's' are called *contractions*. The apostrophe shows that a letter has been left out. In some contractions it shows that a number of letters have been left out.

1. What are the contractions of these words?
   a) is not   d) I am
   b) that is   e) need not
   c) he will   f) should not

34

2. Look over these sentences. Find the contractions and write them in full.
   a) You're going to the dentist today.
   b) Many of them couldn't see the movie.
   c) I'd like to visit the park.
   d) She doesn't often travel to the city.
   e) I see they're over by the stable.

Build-a-word

Using the word 'dust' in a build-a-word game, we would end up with such words as:

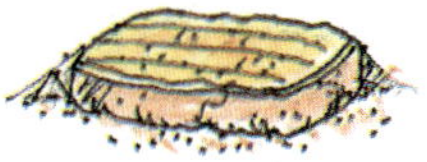

dusted   dusting   dusty
dusts   duster

1. How many other words can you build using these words? Keep a list.
   a) weary
   b) east
   c) realise 
   d) wave
   e) sleep
   f) shine

Hyphenated words

In the poems 'The Teams' and 'Interstate Driver', the poets have used a number of two-part words with a special mark between them.

broad-brimmed   **half-shut**

The mark between them is called a *hyphen*. Words that are written this way are called *hyphenated* words.

1. a) Make a list of all the hyphenated words in the two poems.
   b) What do the words mean?

35

CHECKPOINT 3
Building blocks

Sentence turnaround

Look over this sentence.

The distant goal is won by the power of the green-hide goad.

It can be written another way.

By the power of the green-hide goad the distant goal is won.

Often we turn sentences around this way. Look at this sentence.

She stood at the window all night long.

Turned around it becomes:

At the window all night long she stood.

This is done quite often to give variety to sentences and to make them more interesting.

1. Turn these sentences around.
   a) The car sped off into the distance.
   b) Many of them stayed for several days.
   c) My brothers and sisters waited near the fence.
   d) All the family scrambled onto the boat.
   e) The shopkeepers gathered at the club house.

Sentence parts

Look over this sentence.

A crowd of travellers gathered at the gate.

The first part of the sentence, the part in **bold italics**, is the naming part of the sentence. It names what the sentence is about. The second part of the sentence is the telling part of the sentence. It tells what is said about the naming part.

1. Which are the naming parts of these sentences.
    a) Several of the boys went to the creek.
    b) They visited the old house.
    c) My young sister played in the team.
    d) His grandfather left for America.
    e) The long caravan travelled easily along the highway.
2. Change these sentences so that the naming part is at the end. The first one is done for you.
    a) Several small creatures were in the box.
        In the box were several small creatures.
    b) A large sandy island lay to the south.
    c) Many wild animals lived in the sanctuary.
    d) A bowl of flowers rested on the edge.
    e) The young boy spoke clearly.
    f) My elder brother rested on the bank.

Capitals and full stops

Many poems are written with capitals and full stops used this way.

>**A cloud of dust on the long white road,**
>   **And the teams go creeping on**
>**Inch by inch with the weary load;**
>**And by the power of the green-hide goad**
>   **The distant goal is won.**

Capital letters are used for the start of each new line and a full stop is used at the end of the verse.

In this verse, however, the poet has decided not to use capitals for each new line. He wants us to read it over quickly so that the message of the poem; the speed of transport, is quite clear.

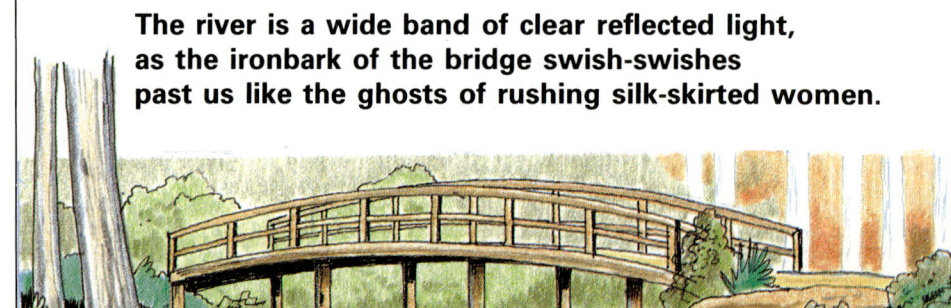

>**The river is a wide band of clear reflected light,**
>**as the ironbark of the bridge swish-swishes**
>**past us like the ghosts of rushing silk-skirted women.**

1. Write the first verse of a poem about a racing car or something else which is fast. Think about where you will put your capitals and full stops.
2. Write the first verse of a poem about something slow and steady, like a tortoise or a boring day at school. Think about where you will put your full stops and capitals.
3. Add more verses to the poem you like best.

CHECKPOINT 4
Action time

Rhyme change

Read this rhyme.

> The lion and the unicorn
>   were fighting for the crown
> The lion beat the unicorn
>   All round the town
>
> Some gave them white bread
>   and some gave them brown
> Some gave them plum-cake
>   And sent them out of town

Now read over the changes that have been made.

> The fox and the wombat
>   Were wrestling for the cup
> The fox chased the wombat
>   Round and down and up
>
> Some gave them white bread
>   and some gave them cakes
> Some gave them ice cream
>   And chased them to the lakes

Notice that only some of the words have been changed. You can see that there are pairs of rhyming words in each verse.

crown — town   brown — town
cup — up   cakes — lakes

1. Read over this rhyme. Can you make changes to this rhyme?

>Old Mother Hubbard
>   Went to the cupboard
>To get her poor dog a bone
>   But when she got there
>The cupboard was bare
>   And so the poor dog had none
>She went to the bakers'
>   To buy him some bread
>But when she came back
>   The poor dog was dead
>She took a clean dish
>   To get him some tripe
>But when she came back
>   He was smoking his pipe

Syllable poems

A syllable poem can look like this.

See	*1 syllable*
The bird	*2 syllables*
It looks out	*3 syllables*
To the left-right	*4 syllables*
Wearily watching	*5 syllables*
Alert and shy	*4 syllables*
Protecting	*3 syllables*
Young ones	*2 syllables*
Look	*1 syllable*

1. Write your own syllable poem. Think of a topic and make your own syllable pattern. As you write, sound out each word and count the syllables.

Acrostic poems

An acrostic poem is a special poem. Read this acrostic poem called the 'Tiger'. Can you see anything special about this type of poem?

Tiger
The animal prince
In thickets and grasslands
Grumbling and searching
Eating where it likes
Ruling its area

1. Make your own acrostic poem. Think of a topic yourself. Make sure the first letter on each line spells out the title of the poem downwards.

CHECKPOINT 5
Moving on

Task 1 Make a collection
Collect a number of acrostic poems. Have each of them rewritten in the centre of a separate page. Illustrate them carefully. Set them up in a photo album or special book. Share your completed book with other classes in your school.

Task 2 Observe and write
Look around your classroom and select an object to write a poem about. Don't worry about rhyme — just let your thoughts turn into words. First, look at the subject carefully because description can make up a large part of your poem. Your ideas will come from:
- looking at the object
- touching the object
- listening, thinking, comparing and remembering.

Task 3 Make a list
Much poetry is made up of vivid descriptions of people, places and things. Let us look a little closer at people. Collect a number of pictures of adults and children from the newspaper. Discuss:
- Facial expressions — do they look happy, sad or alarmed?
- Hand and arm positions — are they relaxed, active or excited?

There are many other words besides 'happy', 'sad', 'alarmed', 'relaxed', 'active' and 'excited'. Make a list of the words you thought out.

UNIT 4
FOCUS   Recipes

Cooking is the way people change raw food into things that look and taste differently. Heat is often used and cold can also be used to alter raw food. Sometimes foods are changed by the way they are mixed together.

There is not only one way to cook. All over the world people have worked out ways to change raw food into something that looks and tastes better. People trying out new ideas, changing the amounts in mixtures, and accidently inventing new things to eat have all altered the ways of cooking.

Read over these recipes. They are examples of some of the different ways that recipes are written.

Recipe 1 — Chocolate fudge

First, put $\frac{3}{4}$ of a ⌣ of 🥛 plus ⌣ of unsweetened chocolate and $\frac{1}{4}$ butter into a 🍲 and melt over a low 🔥 or 🔥. Next, sift ⌣⌣⌣ of powdered 🍚 and add $\frac{1}{2}$ to the melted chocolate.

Now beat in 1 🥚 and 1 🥄 of 🧴 . Then add the other ⌣ of sugar. Add ⌣ of chopped 🥜 and press the fudge into a flat tin lined with foil or waxed paper.

Chill until firm!

Cut into squares and EAT.

44

Recipe 2 — Fairy cakes

This recipe will make enough for about fifteen little cakes. You will need to collect the things listed below before you begin.

An almost full cup of sugar   a heaped cup of self-raising flour   a $\frac{1}{2}$ a cup of milk   a large saucepan and a wooden spoon

patty cake cases   2 eggs   2 tablespoons of butter   space to work

Turn the oven on before you begin. Set the oven on 350 degrees for an electric oven and about 400 degrees for a gas oven.

Step 1.   Melt the butter in the saucepan over a low heat.
Step 2.   Take the pan off the heat and add the sugar.
Step 3.   Break in the eggs and stir well.
Step 4.   Add the flour. Stir the mixture well as the flour is slowly added.
Step 5.   Slowly add the milk, stirring all the time.
Step 6.   Keep stirring until the mixture is smooth. Make sure there are no lumps.
Step 7.   Put large spoonfuls into the patty cake cases.
Step 8.   Place the small cakes on a tray in the middle of the oven and close the door quickly. The small cakes will take about 25 minutes to cook.
Step 9.   Take the cakes from the oven and place on a rack to cool.
Step 10. This is the best step of all. Sample your goodies.

Recipe 3 — Chocolate-chip cookies

Ingredients:

125 g butter
1 cup sugar
$\frac{1}{2}$ teaspoon vanilla

1 egg
$1\frac{3}{4}$ cups self-raising flour
125 g chocolate chips

Method:

Cream butter, sugar and vanilla. Add beaten egg gradually. Mix in flour. Add chocolate chips. Place teaspoonfuls of the mixture on a greased tray and bake in a moderate oven for 10−12 minutes.

CHECKPOINT 1
Discussion time

Comment and answer
1. If you had to choose only one of the recipes to make which one would you choose? Why would you choose that particular recipe?
   a) Because you think it would be the best one to eat.
   b) Because you think the instructions are clearer.
   c) Because you think it would be quicker and easier to make.
   d) All of these reasons.
   e) Some other reason.
2. Which recipe is the easiest to follow? Why do you think this? Discuss your reasons with other class members.
3. In recipe 3 it says to place the greased tray in a 'moderate' oven. What does this mean?
4. When cooking, you must do things in the correct order or sequence. Discuss recipe 1 with your classmates and divide the instructions into steps.
5. In recipe 3 what is the correct sequence of steps to follow?
6. The sequence in these cooking instructions is all jumbled up. Read the instructions and suggest the correct sequence.
   - Clean up all cooking utensils and wipe over the cooking bench.
   - Sample the product you have cooked.
   - Read the recipe.
   - Preheat the oven.
   - Collect together all the utensils and ingredients you will need.
7. In recipe 2, what is the correct sequence for adding the milk, the sugar and the flour?

8. Read this statement and answer the questions below.

All ovens are different so your cooking may take more or less time than the recipe states. Don't open the oven to check until about 5 minutes before your cakes or cookies should be cooked. Cold air makes cakes sink.

   a) What effect does cool air have on cooking cakes?
   b) What causes cakes to sink?
   c) What is the cause of different cooking times for the same recipe?
   d) What would be the effect if all ovens were the same?
   e) What would be the effect if you only cooked your cookies for half the time stated in the recipe?
   f) What causes things to burn and spoil in the oven?

9. Read these statements and say which are true and which are false.
   a) The ingredients in any recipe can be added in any sequence at all.
   b) It is best to put the oven on before you start preparing to cook.
   c) Cooking is the way people change raw food.
   d) Heat is always used in cooking.
   e) Recipes are only really a list of ingredients and a set of instructions.

CHECKPOINT 2
Exploring words

Abbreviations

> Many recipes use abbreviations of one form or another. Recipe 1 uses abbreviations in this form:
>
> 1/2   This abbreviation means 'half a cup'
>
> 2   This abbreviation means 'two eggs'.

1. Find other examples of the abbreviations used in recipes 1, 2 and 3.
2. Search recipe books and find the abbreviations used for these words.
   - a) gram
   - b) kilogram
   - c) tablespoon
   - d) degrees
   - e) minutes
3. Look for other abbreviations. What do they mean?

Word meanings

1. Here are some words that are often found in recipes. What do they mean? Use them in sentences to show that you understand how to use them.
   - a) ingredients
   - b) knead
   - c) fold
   - d) method
   - e) moderate
   - f) blend

Silent letters

> Read over this sentence.
>
> **A *knife* is often used in cooking.**
>
> The word 'knife' has a *silent letter*, the letter 'k'. Silent letters are those that cannot be heard when you say a word out loud.

1. Say these words out loud. Find the silent letter.
   - (a) write
   - (b) gnaw
   - (c) wrap
   - (d) knave
   - (e) wreck
   - (f) knot
   - (g) wrong
   - (h) knob
   - (i) wren
2. Make a list of other words that you know have silent letters.

Synomyms — words that mean the same

> Look at these statements.
>
> **Bread is one of the oldest foods. It is not as *difficult* to make as it sounds.**
>
> **Bread is one of the oldest foods. It is not as *hard* to make as it sounds.**
>
> The words 'hard' and 'difficult' mean the same, or nearly the same, in these statements. They are called *synonyms*.

1. Find the synonyms in the jumble of words below.

   | anxious | yelled | frightened | maybe | powerful |
   | alarmed | perhaps | shouted | strong | concerned |

2. Make a list of at least six pairs of synonyms. Think of words and then try to think of other words that have the same meaning.

CHECKPOINT 3
Building blocks

Verbs — action words

> There are many action words in cooking. Recipes always instruct you to do something.
>
> > ***Stir*** the mixture.
> > ***Add*** the sugar.
> > Now ***break*** the eggs.
> > ***Place*** the tin in the oven and ***cook*** for 20 minutes.
>
> These doing words, or action words, are called *verbs.*

1. Find the verbs in these instructions.
   a) First peel the apple.
   b) Mix the dry ingredients.
   c) On top of the mixture sprinkle coconut.
   d) Grate the cheese.
   e) Wash all the used utensils.

2. The verbs have been left out of these instructions. Supply a suitable verb in each case. There may be many correct answers. Discuss your answers with other class members.
   a) Now slowly _____ the milk, _____ all the time.
   b) _____ the mixture into the cake tin.
   c) _____ them slowly over a low heat.
   d) Shishkebabs can be _____ or _____ on a barbecue.
   e) _____ a spoonful of butter in the pan.

Commas

> Read this sentence.
>
> **All kinds of food can be cut into cubes for cooking in shishkebabs; lamb, beef, bacon, sausage, apple, onion, tomato, green pepper and many others.**
>
> Notice how the comma is used to separate the items in the list of things that can be used in shishkebabs.

51

1. Rewrite this sentence and put in the commas that have been left out.

   You could use any of these flavourings in this recipe; a few drops of vanilla two tablespoons of cocoa a handful of currants or sultanas or a mashed banana.

2. Often other punctuation marks are used to separate items in a recipe. Find as many different types as you can. Display them and discuss them with your classmates and teacher.

Nouns — naming words

1. Remember that naming words are called *nouns*. Find the nouns in this section of a recipe.

   Pancakes
   This recipe will make four big pancakes about the size of dinner plates or lots of small ones.

   You will need:
   - 1 cup of plain flour
   - 1 egg
   - 1 cup of milk
   - $\frac{1}{2}$ teaspoon of salt
   - butter or oil for frying
   - a large mixing bowl, a frying pan, a spoon, an egg slice and a cup

CHECKPOINT 4
Action time

Read and rewrite

1. Read recipe 1 and then rewrite recipe 3 so that it is in a similar format to recipe 1. You might start like this:

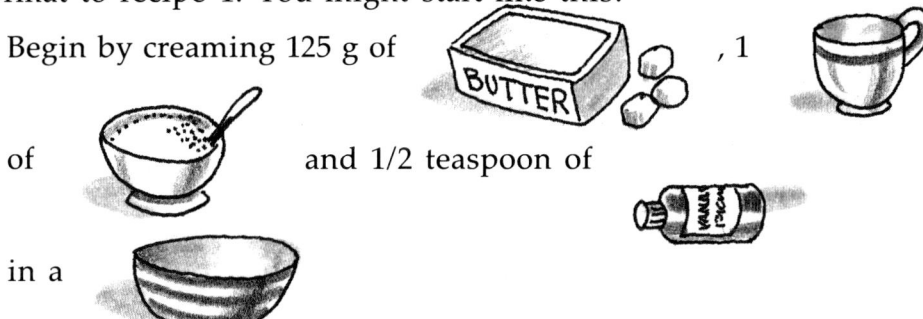

   Begin by creaming 125 g of [butter], 1 [cup] of [sugar] and 1/2 teaspoon of [vanilla] in a [bowl].

2. Find the recipe for coconut ice in a recipe book. Make a list of the ingredients and read the instructions on how to make the sweet. Put away the recipe book and try to remember the instructions you've read. Write out the instructions as you remember them. Have a guess at what you can't remember. Then, check to see how close you were.

Mystery recipe

1. a) These are the ingredients for a mystery recipe. What do you think they will make? (The answer is at the bottom of the page.)
    - 200 g milk chocolate
    - 25 g marshmallow
    - 25 g nut pieces
    - 1 desertspoon cooking oil

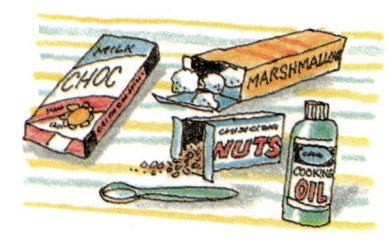

   b) Unfortunately, the instructions on how to make the sweet are out of order. You will have to read and rearrange the steps before you can make the sweet.

   Step 1. Spread half the melted chocolate in a greased cake tin.

   Step 2. Fill the bottom saucepan with water, but not so that it touches the bottom of the bowl.

   Step 3. Cool for at least 8 hours and cut into squares with a knife.

   Step 4. Place the broken chocolate pieces into a double boiler (or a bowl that will fit into a saucepan without touching the bottom).

   Step 5. Grease a small cake tin.

   Step 6. Add the oil and heat gently until the chocolate melts and stir to blend.

   Step 7. Dot the nuts and marshmallows all over and cover with the rest of the chocolate.

Answer: *Rocky road*

CHECKPOINT 5
Moving on

Task 1   Make a recipe rack

You will need:
- a large plastic detergent bottle with an oval or rectangular base.

What to do:

Step 1.   Cut away the top of the bottle leaving 8 centimetres of the bottom section.

Step 2.   Cut out the sides, as shown with the dotted line, making a notch for the recipe card.

Step 3.   Decorate the rack with felt-tip pens to match your kitchen.

Task 2   Start your own recipe book
Collect and paste your favourite recipes into a scrap book. You might like to have different sections in your book. Perhaps cakes, biscuits, sweets, meat dishes, or any others you like. Put a name on each separate section of your book. Decorate and display.

Task 3   List the ingredients
Many different ingredients are used in different types of cooking. For example, if you were cooking sweets, cakes or biscuits, you may use some of the following:

Types of sugar	You might use	You might add
sugar castor sugar brown sugar fine sugar raw sugar	butter margarine cooking oil plain flour self-raising flour	salt colouring flavouring chopped nuts coconut

List all the ingredients you might use if you were cooking a meat dish.

Types of meat	Vegetables	You might add

UNIT 5
FOCUS   News report

Read the news report 'A long road for Lloyd and an L-plate pup'.

A long road for Lloyd and an L-plate pup

MELBOURNE. — When Lloyd Wilson walks into his home town of Rochester on February 26, he will celebrate more than just his 70th birthday.

The northern Victorian town will mark the end of a difficult 1200 kilometre trek for Lloyd and two other swaggies, which will take them over the Blue Mountains and across outback New South Wales.

Lloyd and South Gippsland brothers Peter and Noel Johnson will trek from Sydney to Rochester as part of the Bicentennial celebrations.

The trio — with a combined age of 195 years — will live as tramps, sleeping on the roadside and under bridges and relying on handouts for food.

(continued)

Their belongings will be a swag and tuckerbag on their backs and a billy in hand in true Australian style.

Tagging along, hopefully, will be Lloyd's young pup, Rover.

The Queensland heeler-bull terrier cross pup is just four months old and is still very much a learner.

Lloyd and Rover are often seen trekking around Rochester, in training for next year's trip.

'He's only a young dog, and you don't want to break him on his first journey,' said 69 year-old Lloyd, who will be travelling under the alias Charlie Dunne.

'If the trip is too much for him — he'll only be eight months at the time — then we'll only take him part of the way.'

'He's got two jobs — to guard me at night when I'm asleep and to pull me along during the day when I get tired.'

'No one will want to touch me when I'm asleep because the dog will eat em.'

The retired farmer and ex-serviceman said he was in top shape for the journey, which was designed to commemorate the pioneers of Australia.

The swaggies will pay tribute to events such as the first crossing of the Blue Mountains, Ned Kelly's hold-ups in Jerilderee, and the world blade-shearing record set in 1892.

Courier Mail
Monday, November 2, 1987

CHECKPOINT 1
Discussion time

Comment and answer
1. Make up two 'who?', 'what?', 'when?', 'where?', 'why?' and 'how?' questions about this article. Ask your questions of other class members and discuss the answers they give. Your questions could be like these:
   - Who was going on the journey?
   - Why were they making the trek?
2. Study the portrait of Lloyd and his pup and answer these questions.
   a) How is Lloyd dressed?
   b) Why is the dog wearing an L plate?
   c) What is the billy for?
   d) How old do you think the man is?
   e) What is he carrying over his shoulder?
3. Read these questions and answer them, stating what you think will happen in each case.
   a) Will Lloyd and his mates complete the 1200 kilometre trek?
   b) Will Rover make it all the way?
   c) Who will they meet along the way?
   d) How long do you think the trek will last?
   e) How will people react when they see them along the road?

CHECKPOINT 2
Exploring words

Syllables

Read this sentence out loud and listen carefully to the *italicised* words.

Lloyd and his dog, *Rover*, will *hopefully complete* a *remarkable* and *difficult journey*.

Read it again and listen to the number of *syllables* in each of the *italicised* words. They can be shown like this:

Ro/ver   hope/fully   com/plete   re/mark/able
diff/ic/ult   jour/ney

1. Read these words out loud and mark in where you think the syllable breaks should be.
   a) carpenter
   b) children
   c) swagman
   d) belongings
   e) travelling

Alphabetical order

1. Here is a list of some of the things Lloyd took on his trek. Rewrite the list in alphabetical order.
   tuckerbag,   dog,   billy,   swag,   hat
2. Which letter comes before each of these letters in the alphabet?
   a) X   b) B   c) M   d) P   e) I
3. Which letter comes just after each of these letters?
   a) V   b) L   c) C   d) D   e) T
4. Arrange these names in alphabetical order.
   Steven,   Fiona,   Mark,   Dell,   Adam

5. Crack the code to find the occupations of these five people. When you've found the occupations, arrange them in alphabetical order.

A	B	C	D	E	F	G	H	I	J	K
3	2	17	1	11	10	8	18	14	20	6
L	M	N	O	P	Q	R	S	T	U	V
7	5	21	4	23	9	13	26	12	19	16
W	X	Y	Z							
24	22	15	25							

1;4;17;12;4;13.

21;19;13;26;11.

2;19;14;7;1;11;13.

16;11;12.

12;11;3;17;18;11;13.

CHECKPOINT 3
Building blocks

Proper nouns and capitals

> Did you notice that all the names in the article, 'A long road for Lloyd and an L-plate pup', started with a capital letter?
>
> **Rover   Lloyd   Wilson   Victorian   Blue Mountains**
> **Peter   Noel**
>
> We call these words *proper nouns* because they are the names of people and places. All proper nouns begin with a capital letter.

1. Find some more proper nouns in the focus article.
2. Which of these nouns are proper nouns and should be written with a capital letter?
   a) queensland
   b) swagman
   c) toy
   d) robert
   e) boy
3. Look at this short passage and rewrite it, this time using capitals for the proper nouns.

   > The carson family, with judy and anton, made their way from broken hill towards the south australian border.

Capitals and full stops

1. Here is a news flash that has been written without capital letters and full stops. Can you rewrite it correctly.

   > flash flooding in the kent street area is disrupting afternoon traffic motorists are asked to avoid the area full details in tonight's news

2. Write a news flash to report one of the following. Be sure to punctuate it correctly.
   a) A bank hold-up
   b) A three-car accident in the main street
   c) A bomb scare

Nouns and verbs

1. The words in boxes in this passage are either nouns or verbs. Can you tell which words are nouns and which are verbs?

   [Swaggies moved] from place to [place searching] for [work.] They often [travelled] alone with only a [dog] as a companion. They [were] sometimes [called sundowners] because they [arrived] at a homestead at sundown.

2. Supply suitable nouns or verbs to complete these sentences.
   a) _____ often _____ in the park.
   b) The little _____ _____ his tail when the children arrived home from school.
   c) All the team members _____ as well as they could.
   d) The beautiful _____ that _____ near the wall were roses.
   e) During the _____ the _____ was blown from the _____.

   Not all answers will be the same. Discuss your answers with other class members.

CHECKPOINT 4
Action time

Write a summary
1. Write a summary, about five or six sentences long, of the article 'A long road for Lloyd and an L-plate pup'. These questions might help you to organise your summary:
   - Where was the trek to take place?
     From _____ to _____.
   - Why were Lloyd and his friends making the trip?
   - Where were they going to sleep and how were they going to be fed?
   - What were they taking with them?

Research and write
1. Research and write a short report on the topic: Perhaps the best known of Australian songs is 'Waltzing Matilda'. Include in your report the answers to these questions:
   - Who wrote the words for 'Walting Matilda'?
   - What does the title mean?

Write a description
1. Look at the drawing of Lloyd and Rover and think about words and phrases that could be used to describe them. Then write a short description, only about four or five sentences, to describe Lloyd and his dog. You could describe Lloyd's clothes, beard, hat, billy, swag and tuckerbag. And you could describe Rover's L plate, chain, ears and markings.

Write a short story
1. Imagine that you went on the trek with Lloyd and Rover. Write a short story to tell of your adventures. You could write about where you went, who you met, what the country was like, when you were afraid, when you were happy, what you had to eat, and when you reached the end of your journey.

CHECKPOINT 5
Moving on

Task 1 Tell a story
Imagine that you are Lloyd's battered and blackened old billy. Think of all the stories you could tell about the places you have been and all the strange characters you have met. Tell your story and share it with others.

Task 2 Research and read
There are many stories and poems about outback Australia. Find these stories, books and poems in your school library and read them to your class or group. Find out who wrote the stories, books or poems.
- 'Crooked Mick of the Speewah'
- 'A Bush Christening'
- 'Waltzing Matilda'
- 'The Loaded Dog'
- 'Had Yer Jabs'

'Once a Jolly Swagman'

Task 3 Make a collection
Collect poems, stories and pictures of swaggies and bush characters and display them on a wall chart. Discuss your chart with the class.

UNIT 6
FOCUS Literature

Read this extract from the book *Pigs Might Fly* by Emily Rodda.

Pigs Might Fly

Emily Rodda

'I wish something would happen!' said Rachel. 'Something interesting!'

Afterwards, she would remember what she'd said and how she'd felt, that rainy Saturday morning. If *only* something unlikely or unexpected would happen for a change. Something exciting; something wonderful.

'May-be it will!' her father said. 'And pigs might fly!'

But he was only teasing. Pigs can't fly. Can they?

Rachel blinked. Something had happened to the light. It had spread, and brightened. Everything looked pale green. She blinked again and looked slowly around. This wasn't right! Her room had disappeared. Her bed had disappeared. She was in the middle of a broad, green field, in her pyjamas, sitting astride a —

The unicorn turned its head and looked at her gravely. It snorted softly. Its golden horn glittered in the sunlight, its white mane stirred gently in the breeze.

'Oh, no!' whispered Rachel. 'What have I done?'

The great muscles in the unicorn's back twitched and it began to walk slowly forward, placing its feet gently on the tussocky green grass.

Rachel had only ridden a horse once before — and that was a Shetland pony. Only half a horse compared with this huge creature. She clutched desperately at the silky mane and hung on tightly with her knees. What else could she do? She couldn't possibly jump off. It was a long way to the ground.

The unicorn moved on quietly. And then Rachel heard the first, faint grunting. She knew where it was coming from, but at first she just couldn't bring herself to look. She screwed up her eyes and counted to ten. Then she opened one eye. Oh, no! She quickly shut it again. But it was no good. Seeing was believing, and she had to know the worst. She held on tightly to the unicorn's mane, counted to ten again, gritted her teeth, and looked up into the blue sky.

The pigs were there, sailing plumply, pinkly, just above her, grunting softly to themselves. As she watched, one rolled over in a somersault and kicked its trotters at the sun with a little squeak of pleasure.

The unicorn pricked its ears and began to trot. Rachel held on grimly, bouncing on the broad, slippery back. No point in calling out — she couldn't see a single living creature who might help her. The pigs were having far too good a time even to notice she was there. She was in a strange field, in her pyjamas, riding on a unicorn!

'This must be a dream,' thought Rachel suddenly. 'Of course! That means I'll wake up soon, and there's nothing to worry about. It doesn't feel like a dream, but these things just don't happen in real life, so it must be.' This thought comforted her very much. She noticed her drink bottle sticking out of her pyjama pocket. Somehow that comforted her too. Something from home. What a shame it was empty. Her fright had made her thirsty.

The unicorn nickered warningly and quickened its pace. Rachel looked over its arching neck and saw that it had reached the crest of a hill and was heading for a small white house tucked away in the valley below. A pink blob bobbed around in the sky above the house. Another pig, for heaven's sake! And even as she watched she saw that the wind was bringing more of them into view, tumbling and rolling. Little pigs, squealing and squeaking in excitement, medium-sized pigs, their legs spread out blissfully to catch the cool breeze, a few very big, whiskery old pigs, sailing along in majestic fashion, looking neither to right nor left. One great pig, the grandfather of all pigs, stood massively on the hillside, watching them with wise little eyes.

CHECKPOINT 1
Discussion time

Comment and answer
1. What do you think will happen next to Rachel and the unicorn?
2. If you go to sleep thinking about something, what often happens?
3. The unicorn is an animal that often appears in myths and legends. Find other stories about the unicorn.
4. Rachel noticed her drink bottle and it comforted her. How could this be a comfort to her? What things do you have that are a comfort to you?
5. Predict what will happen when Rachel wakes from her dream.
6. Are these statements true or false?
    a) Rachel imagined that she was riding on a unicorn surrounded by flying pigs.
    b) Unicorns are real animals that lived many years ago.
    c) The unicorns in myths and legends always have a single horn between their eyes.
    d) 'Pigs might fly' is really a saying that means something is unlikely to happen.
    e) Rachel really rode on a unicorn and saw flying pigs.
7. Do you think dreams can come true?
8. In your opinion, what was the best dream you ever had? Share it with your classmates.
9. Some people say that if you eat too much just before you go to sleep you will have nightmares. What is your opinion?
10. People have claimed that they have dreamt about things that were going to happen in the future. Could this be correct?
11. There are many stories from the Aboriginal dreamtime. How can these stories be explained?

CHECKPOINT 2
Exploring words

Singular and plural

> Many of the words from the extract from *Pigs Might Fly* become plurals when 's' is added.
>
>   **dream — dreams**   **pig — pigs**   **unicorn — unicorns**
>
> Other words, which end in 'y' become plurals when the final 'y' is changed to 'i' and 'es' is added.
>
>   **pony — ponies**   **party — parties**   **duty — duties**

1. Change these singular words to plurals.
   - a) baby
   - b) jelly
   - c) fairy
   - d) copy
   - e) hobby
2. Now change these singular words to plurals.
   - a) girl
   - b) berry
   - c) kitten
   - d) cow
   - e) dolly

Word families

> Word families can be made by adding different endings to a word. The word family that can be made by building on the word 'blink' includes the words:
>
>   **blink   blinks   blinked   blinking**

1. Use these verbs from the extract of the story *Pigs Might Fly* to build word families.
   - a) snort   _____s   _____ed   _____ing
   - b) walk   _____s   _____ed   _____ing

    c) pick   ____s   ____ed   ____ing
    d) jump   ____s   ____ed   ____ing
    e) kick   ____s   ____ed   ____ing

2. Build word families with these words. Take special care with the spelling.
   - a) squeal
   - b) comfort
   - c) watch
   - d) catch
   - e) count

Build-a-word

> Words can be built by adding letter blends to word stems. If the blend 'str' is added to the stem 'eam', 'stream' is created.

1. Add the 'str' blend to these word stems.
   - a) __ipe
   - b) __ait
   - c) __and
   - d) __oke
   - e) __ike
2. Find other word stems that you can add to the 'str' blend.

Suffixes

> Read this sentence from *Pigs Might Fly*.
>
> **The unicorn moved on *quietly*.**
>
> The 'ly' in the word **quietly** is called a *suffix*. It is a very common suffix.

1. Use the suffux 'ly' to form new words from these words.
   - a) sudden
   - b) happy
   - c) weary
   - d) first
   - e) slow
2. What do you think the suffix 'ly' means?

CHECKPOINT 3
Building blocks

Direct speech

1. This sentence appears in the extract from *Pigs Might Fly*.

    'Oh, no,' whispered Rachel.

    a) What were the words that Rachel actually spoke?
    b) Can you find any other places in the focus story where you can see the actual words spoken by Rachel?
    c) How do you know they are the exact words that she spoke?
    d) Can you find out the name that is given to the marks that show the exact words spoken?

2. Here is another sentence taken from *Pigs Might Fly*. It has been written without the speech marks. Could you rewrite it showing the speech marks?

    I suppose if I did fall I'd wake up she thought to herself.

Questions and answers

1. Read these sentences. Some are questions and some are answers.

    - It's in the bottom drawer.
    - At about half past seven.
    - Where did you put the cotton?
    - When will it be time for school?
    - I'm nine years old.
    - After you've eaten your breakfast and dressed.
    - How old are you?
    - What time do you have breakfast?

    a) Which sentences are questions? How do you know? There may be more than one reason.
    b) Which sentences are answers? How do you know?
    c) Match up each question with an answer that makes sense.

2. Write some questions and answers on pieces of card and jumble them up. Exchange them with a friend who has done the same. See if you can ask and answer your friend's set of cards.

Broken sentences

1. Look at the way these sentences have been broken up into three separate pieces or chunks.

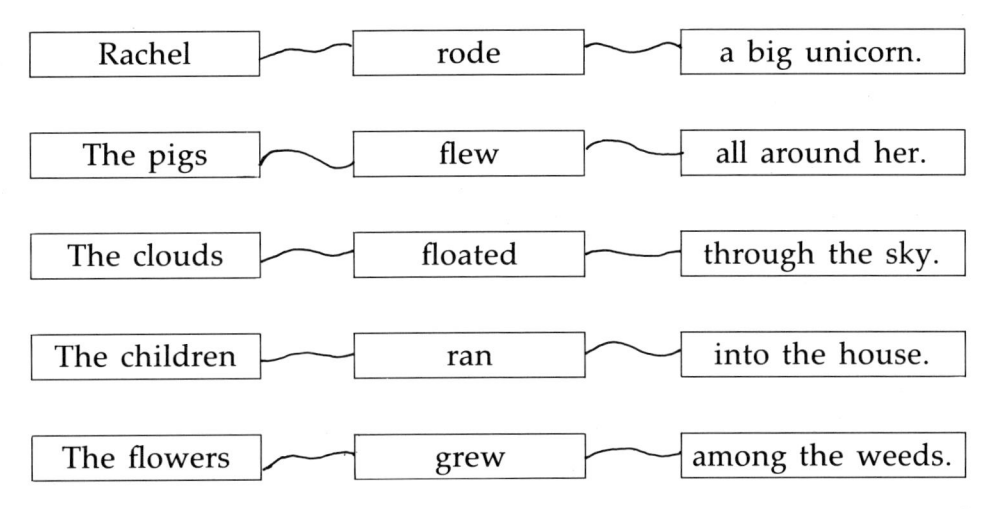

| Rachel | rode | a big unicorn. |

| The pigs | flew | all around her. |

| The clouds | floated | through the sky. |

| The children | ran | into the house. |

| The flowers | grew | among the weeds. |

a) What would happen if the strings between the chunks of language were cut?

b) How many different ways could pieces be put back together to make sense?
Like this:

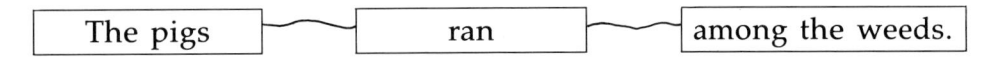

| The pigs | ran | among the weeds. |

c) How many nonsense sentences could you make?
Like this:

| The children | grew | a big unicorn. |

d) Put these pieces of language onto separate cards and have some fun mixing and matching.

e) Record the sentences that make sense and those that are nonsense.

73

CHECKPOINT 4
Action time

Finish the story

1. Here is a story for you to finish.

   Tracey had just climbed into bed after a wonderful birthday party. She had received gifts from her parents and friends and an exciting book from the lady next door. She closed her eyes and drifted off into a peaceful sleep.

   Suddenly her room was filled with a pale green light and as she blinked and rubbed her eyes all her fairy book characters came into view.

   What happened next?

Replace-a-word

Very often the word 'nice' is used to describe all sorts of things. It is one of the most over-used words in our language. Let's put it to rest for a while and use other words instead.

1. Rewrite this sentence and replace the word 'nice'.

   That was a *nice* party we had.

   > pleasant   wonderful   fine   lovely
   > friendly   beaut   good   fantastic

2. Find an alternate word for *nice* in this sentence.

   I think that John is a *nice* boy.

   > friendly   fine   warm-hearted   kind
   > sympathetic   interesting   pleasant
   > attractive   charming

3. Substitute other words for *nice* in this sentence.

A *nice* girl wouldn't behave like that.

> well-brought-up   lady-like   gentle
> caring   well-bred   respectable

Write a story
1. In the story *Pigs Might Fly*, Rachel had a dream about flying pigs. Try writing a story telling about a strange dream you have had. It might be about flying cars or singing post boxes or some other strange thing.

Describe-a-sentence

Read this sentence about a stream.

The stream tinkled and chattered over well-smoothed stones as it wandered towards the large river.

1. Write a descriptive sentence about each of these.
    a) a butterfly
    b) a busy bee
    c) a cat fight
    d) a hungry mouse

CHECKPOINT 5
Moving on

Task 1 Read and illustrate
Read and illustrate this poem.

If Pigs Could Fly

If pigs could fly, I'd fly a pig
To foreign countries small and big —
To Italy and Spain
To Austria, where cowbells ring
To Germany, where people sing —
And then come home again.

I'd see the Ganges and the Nile;
I'd visit Madagascar's Isle,
And Persia and Peru.
People would say they'd never seen
So odd, so strange, an air-machine
As that on which I flew.

Why, everyone would raise a shout
To see his trotters and his snout
Come floating from the sky;
And I would be a famous star
Well known in countries near and far —
If only pigs could fly

James Reeves

Task 2 Reasearch some myths
- The unicorn is a mythical animal. Can you find other stories about unicorns?
- What can you find out about Pegasus the flying horse?
- Greek myths and legends tell the story of Icarus. Find out what this story is about.

Task 3 Create and make
- Create a collage with flying animals to display for the class to see.
- Make mobiles to hang in your room of 'flying animals'.
- Make model 'flying saucers' to decorate and display.
- Make a timeline showing important events in the history of flight.

UNIT 7
FOCUS
Diaries, logs and journals

Diaries, logs and journals are day-by-day records of things that someone has seen or done. Read these two diary entries. The first is a record of Robinson Crusoe's eighth day on a remote island after his ship has been wrecked and his companions drowned. The second was written by Bidu, an American girl who went with her family on a four month trip to Australia and Asia. These entries are the first two days of her trek into Nepal, north of India.

Robinson Crusoe
Daniel Defoe

Eighth day
Yesterday I brought back from the ship a quantity of tools, a drill, a dozen hatchets, a grind-stone for sharpening, iron crowbars, a large bag of nails and rivets; with sails, ropes, poles, two more barrels of powder, a box of musket balls, seven muskets, a third shotgun, lead, a hammock, a mattress, blankets, clothes and great-coats. I thought I had rescued nearly all that was on board. But I was wrong, for today, returning from a trip to the wreck that almost cost me dear — the wind having risen, I capsized with my whole load in the middle of the creek — I saw Japp, the captain's dog, come bounding joyfully along, an Irish setter I had thought drowned with the crew. I think that the poor beast, swept away by the current, had landed on the island much farther away, and had difficulty in finding me. This evening I pitched a little tent with the poles and sail-cloth, under which I spread out my bed. I have piled up all my riches in a shelter from the rain that was threatening. My dog snores at my feet, I have dined on a bit of dried meat and a ship's biscuit, and in spite of the rising wind I am prepared to pass a good night.

Bidu's journal

30 November
Today we began our trek! We got up early and took a bus to Pokhara, where we started walking. The first part of the trail was level, and the morning passed quickly.

We stopped for lunch, and I had the best corn bread I've ever tasted. Then the trail went uphill, and walking was more difficult. But by dinner time we had made it to the town of Naudanda, where we are spending the night.

It is unbelievable. I expected to be sleeping on straw mats. Instead, I have a soft mattress, and there is electricity!

For dinner I tried *dhal bhat*, rice-and-bean soup. It was a little spicy but good. Then I got ready for bed — it was only seven-thirty, but I was very tired.

1 December
The first thing I saw when I opened my window was — mountains. Beautiful!

After breakfast we began trekking. When we stopped for lunch, I had really great curd with corn bread. Then we went down-hill for an hour. It was quite steep and whenever I stopped, my legs started shaking. Finally we reached the inn at Birethanti.

There are no lights here, so we all use candles. I got into bed right after dinner. Then I started to cry. I kept thinking about my dog, Hobbit, who had died just before we left California. I wanted to throw something down the mountain in her memory, but I hadn't brought anything that had special meaning for her. My mom came in my room and stayed with me awhile. She suggested throwing a rock down the mountain, because Hobbit had loved chasing rocks. I kept crying even after my mom left. I really miss my dog.

CHECKPOINT 1
Discussion time

Comment and answer
1. What is the main idea in Robinson Crusoe's eighth day entry?
   a) He was very lucky to find the Irish setter.
   b) Although he had many problems ahead he was pleased with what he had done.
   c) When he was returning from the wreck he capsized the boat in the middle of the creek.
2. Arrange these sentences in the correct sequence.
   a) The dog was snoring at Robinson Crusoe's feet.
   b) All the riches were piled up in a shelter.
   c) The boat capsized in the creek.
   d) A little tent with poles and sail-cloth was set up.
3. a) Do you think that all the items Crusoe brought back from the wreck were useful?
   b) How would each of these items help him to survive on the island?
4. Why do you think he was satisfied with what he had done?
5. What is the main idea in Bidu's 30 November entry?
   a) She was glad to get to bed even though it was only 7.30 pm.
   b) The day was more interesting than she had expected.
   c) The foods that she tasted were quite different.
6. Which three foods are mentioned in the extract from Bidu's journal?
7. Is this statement true? Explain.

   Robinson Crusoe's entries record things seen and done. Bidu's entries record things seen and done and also include feelings of happiness and sadness.

8. Imagine if, on the first night out, Bidu had to stay in a place with no lights. Do you think that it would have made any difference to either of the entries she wrote?

CHECKPOINT 2
Exploring words

Writers and others

1. Look over these names for people who have much to do with books. Match the words and the the meanings below.

    a) printer   d) illustrator
    b) novelist   e) editor
    c) publisher   f) author

- one who writes novels
- one who checks over the original work
- one who writes
- one who prepares drawings
- one who has the book printed
- one who has the book produced

Word opposites — antonyms

Let's look at some more words and their opposites.

wrong — right
risen — fallen
under — over

Words that are opposite in meaning are called *antonyms*.

1. Can you write the antonyms of these words?
    a) good   f) soft
    b) quickly   g) fruitless
    c) difficult   h) uphill
    d) early   i) beautiful
    e) best

82

Double words — compound words

> Two words joined together can make a new word.
>
> **Try some of this *pineapple*.**
>
> The words formed when two other words are joined are called *compound* words.

1. Read over the Robinson Crusoe diary entry. There are several compound words. Find them and use them to complete the sentences below.
    a) The _____ was used to sharpen the knives.
    b) They used _____ to dig the holes.
    c) The _____ was loaded carefully.
    d) The _____ were very warm.
    e) The huge flag was made from _____.
    f) The group walked wearily _____ for many hours.
    g) After _____ the climbers set out.
    h) The _____ ski run was very fast.

Words with apostrophes — contractions

> Words which have been shortened and which have an apostrophe showing that some of the letters have been left out are called *contractions*. Words such as 'isn't', the short form of 'is not', are contractions.

1. What are the contractions of these words?
    a) I am
    b) would not
    c) he will
    d) they will
    e) you will
    f) what is
2. Look over these sentences. Find the contractions that have been used and write them out in full.
    a) They've gone to the shop.
    b) She'll visit her sister.
    c) He doesn't play in the yard.
    d) There's a wisp of smoke near the shop.
    e) What's she doing over there?

CHECKPOINT 3
Building blocks

Missing words
1. Look over this log. It is the log of a boy living on an island. A number of words have been left out of the log. Can you replace them so that the log makes sense? When you have done so, identify the words as nouns or verbs.

   Wednesday 4 April
   This morning _____ and his sister visited us. They had come from the _____. We _____ _____ on the _____ near the cliff. They brought their _____ called _____. He had lots of _____ as well.

   Thursday 5 April
   A big _____ came up this morning. The rain _____ down for about three _____. I liked watching the raindrops bouncing on top of the _____ in the bay. The rain was so thick I could only see about fifty _____ in any direction.

   Friday 6 April
   A _____ of Dad's brought his _____ into the bay this morning. We _____ in his boat to Iffley rocks. The tide was out. We _____ great _____. I caught seven _____. Dad caught a _____. It was over forty _____ in length.

Add a phrase
1. Read over this diary entry. Through the entry you will see **. At these points, add a phrase that adds to the meaning of the sentence. The phrase can be one that describes something, or it could be a phrase that tells how, when, or where.

   Dear Diary,
   Yesterday I had a really good day. We went to the beach **. It was fine and hot. We climbed the trees **. Out on the beach ** we built a great castle. I dug a deep channel **. My little brother Dirk filled it **. Then he stumbled over and broke the walls **. It was a mess. Later ** we played ** in the water. It was a great day!

Capitals and full stops

1. Read over these diary entries. There are several words which need capital letters. Full stops are needed in some places as well. Where should the capitals and full stops be placed?

   Mon. 11
   I saw vicki at the movies
   It was a top show it was called the black stallion after the show we went shopping with vicki's sister lisa

   Tue. 12
   Raining! could hardly see across the road
   Mum said I should tidy my room
   I decided to clean up a bit after lunch
   I rang tammy and had a good chat

   Wed. 13
   Raining again!
   I went with mum to aunt cathy's place
   we helped them unpack their gear after they came back from sydney
   The fire in the fireplace made it nice and cosy

CHECKPOINT 4
Action time

Drawings and diary entries
1. Here's a series of time pictures. Next to the first picture is a diary entry. Imagine you were writing the diary entries for each of the remaining pictures. These entries must be written in such a way that you are observing or taking part in the action.

Today we went to Bell's beach. It was very hot. Sharon and I ran along to the rocks.

Logs and notes

1. Melissa likes to keep a log of day-to-day happenings. Sometimes she simply jots down a few notes and then at the weekend expands the notes into complete sentences. These are her notes for five school days. Can you expand the notes and make them into complete sentences?

    Monday 2.4.89
    Good day — netball practice — Sally and I picked — went to Jenny's on way home

    Tuesday 3.4.89
    Forgot my homework again — more trouble — Mrs Allen gave me extra work — home early — needed to finish project

    Wednesday 4.4.89
    Raining nearly all day — no lunch hour play — home soaking wet — luckily Mum was at the shop — changed quickly

    Thursday 5.4.89
    Never going to stop raining — got in some netball practice — more practice after school — home late

    Friday 6.4.89
    Maths groups today — measuring in playground — pretty messy after rain — afternoon games — great

Thoughts and feelings

> Events and happenings are important in diaries, logs and journals. Thoughts and feelings are also important. They are often written in journals using interesting descriptive words and phrases.

1. Jot down your thoughts and feelings on the following — two or three sentences will do.
    a) an ideal holiday spot
    b) favourite foods
    c) special television shows you never miss
2. Share your thoughts and feelings with others in your class.

CHECKPOINT 5
Moving on

Task 1 Just pretend
Imagine you were stranded in space. How could this happen? Where are you? How are you moving? How are you trying to contact others who may help you? What day-to-day problems do you have? Discuss this situation with others.

Prepare an imaginary log of the days leading up to you being stranded *or* the first few days after you were stranded. Include the events and happenings, and your thoughts and feelings.

Task 2 Compare diaries, logs and journals in literature
There may be several examples of diaries, logs or journals in your library. Set them out for a classroom display. Compare the different types and writing styles.

Task 3 Make a collection
Collect several different kinds of diaries sold at newsagents. What differences can you notice? Many diaries contain information as well as leaving room for entries. What sort of information? Why would this information be useful? Would all the information be useful to all people? Discuss these points.

UNIT 8
FOCUS   Advertisements

Cuddly Cat advertisement

BUY ME NOW!!

HI! I'M CUDDLY CAT. BE MY FRIEND; I'LL BE YOURS.

CUDDLY CAT

SPECIAL INTRODUCTORY PRICE ONLY $19.95 EACH

CUDDLY CAT CAN TALK! ANYTHING YOU SAY CUDDLY CAN REPEAT FOR YOU. THIS CUDDLY COMPANION NEEDS YOU AS A FRIEND. LOVABLE AND TALKATIVE, YOU'LL LOVE CUDDLY CAT

DON'T WAIT!

AVAILABLE FROM GOOD TOY SHOPS AND DEPARTMENT STORES NEAR YOU!

Jay's Joggers advertisement

KNOWN TO BE TOPS!

JAY'S JOGGERS
FOR ACTIVE BOYS AND GIRLS

Tony Rafton, son of ex-ironman champ, Mark Rafton, knows that Jay's Joggers are excellent.

RUNNING-JUMPING-HURDLING ACTION SPORTS
OR FOR CASUAL WEAR.
ALL RUBBER, STRONG-GRIP SOLES.
STRONG TOPS AND LACES.
THE LATEST IN COLOURS.
THE STYLE FOR TODAY.

$19.50

✶ ✶ ✶ ✶ ✶
INTRODUCTORY OFFER
For free sports star cards with each pair purchased this month.

CHECKPOINT 1
Discussion time

Comments and answers
1. Are the following statements true or false?
   a) The talking cat advertisement tells us that the cat can repeat anything spoken to it.
   b) The cat is approximately 30 centimetres high.
   c) The cat is being sold at a special introductory price.
   d) There is a special offer on the joggers if you purchase them this month.
   e) The name of a famous sportsperson is being used to advertise the joggers.
2. Advertisers often use words in advertisements to give you good feelings about a product.
   a) Which words in the cat advertisements are 'good' words?
   b) Which words in the joggers advertisements have been put in to give an idea of active sports?
3. Advertisers often try to explain that by buying quickly you will receive a special offer.
   a) What is the special offer in the cat advertisement?
   b) What is the special offer in the joggers advertisement?
4. Why do you think a picture of the cat was used in the cat advertisement?
5. Why do you think the boy, Tony Rafton, was chosen to be in the joggers advertisement?
6. What is your opinion on these statements?
   a) If you buy something because someone famous says it is good the product is sure to be a good one.
   b) If you do not buy at the special introductory price it will cost more later on.
   c) Different products need different 'good' words used in them.

CHECKPOINT 2
Exploring words

Advertisers' words
1. Read over these sentences used to advertise food products. Which 'good' words have been used to attract the reader? Make a list of them.
    a) Lime ice-curls with that great, tangy, South Sea Island taste.
    b) Delicious, mouthwatering, golden muffins; fresh and hot.
    c) Natural, energy-building muesli blocks for active people.
    d) Anderson's Corn Bran: a nourishing, sustaining, and appetising cereal.
2. Now add to the list any other words you have heard or seen that are used to sell food products.

Words and phrases

Look over these two sentences.

Corn Bran is a *nourishing* cereal.
Corn Bran is a cereal *full of nourishment*.

The word 'nourishing' is a *describing* word.
The phrase 'full of nourishment' really means the same as 'nourishing'.

1. Read over these sentences. Can you change the *italicised* phrase to a single word?
    a) Muesli blocks are *full of goodness*.
    b) These oranges are *full of juice*.
    c) Try these crumpets *with a delicious flavour*.

Alphabetical order

> Remember that placing things in alphabetical order means looking at the first letter of each word. Then you must think of the order of the alphabet and decide which word comes first, second and so on.

1. Look at this list of advertised foods. Arrange the foods in alphabetical order.
    cream, jam, muesli, ice-cream, oranges, wheat-flakes, pies, salad-rolls
2. Which of the three words on each line would come first in a dictionary?
    a) black, truck, lunch
    b) elephant, cupboard, arena
    c) needle, position, which
3. Set out these names in alphabetical order.
    Jane, Alison, Yvonne, Mark, Steve, Brett, Carl, Wendy

4. Look at these describing words. Arrange them in alphabetical order.
    delicious, pleasant, tangy, natural, great, nourishing, appetising

CHECKPOINT 3
Building blocks

Describing words — adjectives

Advertisements use many describing words. Words which tell about other words or describe things are called adjectives. They describe or tell about nouns. Look at these adjectives and nouns.

adjectives   nouns
delicious food
nourishing cereal
long-wearing joggers
fresh fruit

1. Match these nouns with adjectives to suit them.
   a) _____ watch
   b) _____ suit
   c) _____ lemon
   d) _____ saucepans
   e) _____ house
   f) _____ diamond
2. Match these adjectives with nouns to suit them.
   a) luscious _____
   b) faithful _____
   c) dreary _____
   d) friendly _____
   e) sharp _____
   f) wonderful _____
3. Some adjectives tell which colour while others tell how many. Which words in these sentences are adjectives?
   a) Several chestnut horses were in the field.
   b) The seven girls wore red flowers.
   c) Twenty children can eat many cakes.
4. Sometimes several adjectives can be used to describe one noun.
   a) Some bright young person invented the machine.
   b) I have seen many beautiful young ponies.
   c) The shop sold few sweet juicy pears.

Adjectives and phrases

Sometimes an adjective can be replaced with a group of words which mean the same. Look over these.

Here is a *beautiful* painting.
Here is a painting *of great beauty*.

The adjective 'beautiful' was changed to the phrase 'of great beauty'. The sentence still means the same.

1. Can you change the *italicised* adjective into a phrase which means the same?
   a) This is a *dangerous* place.
   b) Take the *steel* box away.
   c) The watermelons were *juicy*.
   d) *Australian* meat is sold overseas.
   e) The *golden-haired* girl played well.

Capitals and full stops

1. Read over these parts of advertisements. The product names and some other nouns need capital letters. Full stops are also needed in some places. Where should the capitals and full stops be placed?
   a) don't forget to buy one of our new line of chocolates they're the best thing in town
   b) jane and alison always wear spot-on hairbands they are the latest and the brightest
   c) fly first class to hong kong by cathay pacific it's the airline where you arrive in better shape

CHECKPOINT 4
Action time

Advertisements that sell
1. Reread the Cuddly Cat and Jay's Joggers advertisements in this unit. Notice the 'good' words that are used.
2. Advertisements need to be set up for two new products.

   Maxi Truck: a new steel-bodied toy that can do many things — at $17.95 each

   BB's Tops: great new cool-weather tops for boys and girls — at $11.90 each

   a) Discuss these points.
      - Which 'good' words could be used to help sell these products?
      - Which other words and phrases could be used?
      - What illustrations would be best for these two advertisements?
   b) Now complete the task by preparing completed advertisements for these two products.

Posters

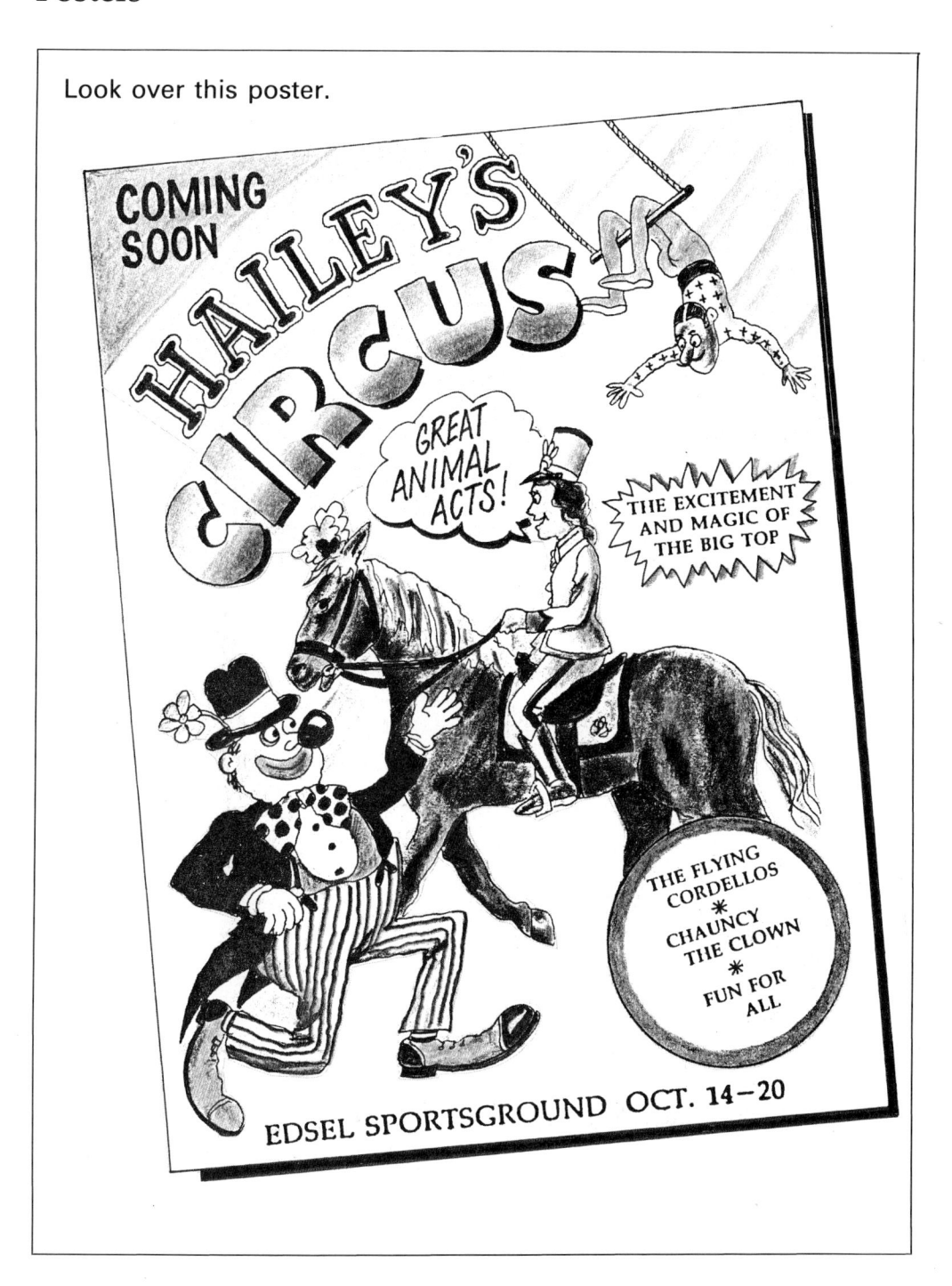

Look over this poster.

Notice that:
- The illustrations are large to attract attention
- Many words are in bold type to stand out
- There are not too many words and no long sentences.

Posters designed this way have a good chance of being noticed. Once again 'good' words were used.

1. Prepare a poster to advertise:
    - The Mopheads — a new rock and roll band
    - Austral Airlines.

    First decide on the illustrations you need. Then decide which 'good' words and which short phrases will attract attention. Don't forget to include any other information needed.

Newspaper advertisements
1. Look over this half-completed advertisement. Discuss how it could be completed to sell the product.

FOR SALE

SeaView

Luxury Apartments

CHECKPOINT 5
Moving on

Task 1   Make a collection
Make a collection of advertisements from newspapers and magazines. Select those advertisements which are advertising a single product or set of products, not the advertisements for a large range of products from the one store or groups of stores. Display these advertisements. Discuss and provide answers to these questions about each advertisement.
- What is the product being advertised?
- Has the advertisement been designed to attract any particular age group — young children, teenagers, parents, grandparents?
- What are you being told about the product?
- Which 'good' words have been used to help promote the product?

Task 2   Tape radio advertisements
Collect several radio advertisements on tape. Discuss and provide answers for the same set of questions as in Task 1. Some radio advertisements have two or more people involved in them. Listen for two or three different voices. Act them out.

Task 3   Compare television commercials
Choose two or three commercials that have been produced to advertise the same sort of product. Compare and discuss these questions.
- What is the product being advertised?
- How has each advertiser tried to promote the product?
- Which words and phrases have been used to add appeal to each product?

UNIT 9
FOCUS　　　　　　Article

Read the article, 'The feathertail glider'.

The feathertail glider

The feathertail glider is a tiny marsupial member of the possum family. At night, in areas of southern Queensland, New South Wales, Victoria and South Australia this tiny animal can be seen, gliding between trees and looking like a small bat.

The feathertail glider is a nocturnal animal; it sleeps during the day and searches for its food after dark. Its main foods are insects and nectar from plants.

When it is first born its little hairless body is smaller than a 2 cent piece. It stays in its mother's pouch until it is too large and heavy for her to carry. At about 4 months of age it is ready to leave the pouch. Each female glider can produce three or four young in a year.

An adult feathertail glider is about 16 centmetres long. Half of this length is body and the rest is tail. Flaps of skin join the front and back legs of the glider. When it jumps from tree to tree it spreads its legs and this stretches the flaps of skin between its legs and makes it look like a small kite gliding through the air. It uses its long feathery tail as a rudder to guide the direction of its glide.

The feathertail builds a ball-shaped nest of twigs and leaves in hollows in the limbs of trees.

This beautiful and harmless little animal can hang from a tree branch by its tail, just like a possum, as it feeds. Unfortunately, feathertail gliders have many predators (enemies) including cats, foxes, goannas and people. People are perhaps the glider's main predator because they often, thoughtlessly, destroy the trees and the bushland which are vital to this gentle creature's survival.

CHECKPOINT 1
Discussion time

Comment and answer
1. Where can the feathertail glider be found?
2. What is meant when the animal is described as a marsupial?
3. How does the feathertail 'fly' from tree to tree?
4. What are the main foods of the feathertail glider?
5. Why do you think foxes, goannas and cats could be dangerous to the feathertails?
6. Discuss these statements and decide if they are true or false.
    a) The feathertail glider is found only in the far northwest of Australia.
    b) The female feathertail only has one baby each year.
    c) The feathertail glider uses its long tail as a rudder when it glides from tree to tree.
    d) The feathertail is not able to hang by its tail like other possums.
    e) Cats and goannas are predators of the small glider.
7. What do you think was the main idea of the article?
    a) That glider possums glide and do not 'fly'.
    b) That feathertail gliders build a ball-shaped nest of twigs and leaves.
    c) To inform you of the feathertail glider's habits and arouse your interest.
8. Study this paragraph:

    The birdlife and animal life in many areas of Australia has been destroyed by the development of cities and factories. We must plan carefully before we destroy what is left. We all have a part to play to ensure that the wildlife of our country will survive.

    a) Which sentence do *you* think is the main idea of this paragraph? Others may pick a different sentence.
    b) Explain why you picked the sentence you did and listen to the reasons others picked a different sentence.

9. Is there an area near your school or home where bushland has been cleared? If so, answer these questions.
   a) What birds and animals have been forced to find a new home?
   b) What should be done before any area of bushland is cleared to make way for factories or housing developments?
   c) What can be done to save the homes of our native birds and animals or to create new homes if bushland is destroyed?

CHECKPOINT 2
Exploring words

Singular and plural

> Some words become plurals when 'es' is added. 
>
> **fox — foxes** 
>
> Some words become plurals when the 'f' in them is changed to a 'v' and 'es' is added. 
>
> **calf — calves** 
>
> Some words can be singular or plural, depending on how they are used
>
> **fish — fish   sheep — sheep**

1. Make these words plurals.
   a) box
   b) church
   c) glass
   d) match
   e) bush
2. Find some more words that become plurals when you add 'es'.
3. Make these words plurals.
   a) leaf
   b) thief
   c) wife
   d) shelf
   e) knife
4. Find some more words that form plurals when you change the 'f' to 'v' and add 'es'.
5. Find some more words that can be either singular or plural.

Build-a-word

Many words are made up of a *prefix*, a *stem*, and a *suffix*. Look at this word.

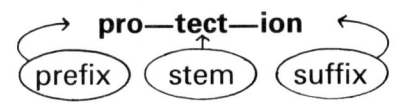

pro—tect—ion
(prefix) (stem) (suffix)

These words use the same prefix and suffix but have a different stem.

pro—duct—ion   pro—mot—ion   pro—fess—ion

1. Find other words that have the pattern pro—|stem|—ion.
2. What do you think the prefix 'pro' means?
3. What do you think the suffix 'ion' means?

Grouping
1. The names of ten animals and their young have been jumbled. List them correctly under the headings 'adult' and 'young'.

pig   duck   lion   deer   cat   piglet
fawn   cub   kitten   duckling

2. Make a list of ten more animals and their young.
3. In each of these lists there is something that does not belong. Find it and explain why it does not belong in the list. There may be more than one reason or more than one correct answer. The first one has been done for you.
   a) cat, dog, horse, bird
      Bird does not belong because all the others have four legs. Horse does not belong because all the others are common household pets.
   b) eagle, emu, sparrow, magpie
   c) ant, ladybird, spider, beetle
   d) car, truck, lorry, bike
   e) plane, car, bus, train

   Discuss your answers and reasons and listen to the answers and reasons from your class members.

CHECKPOINT 3
Building blocks

Lists with dashes and commas

Look at this list of items to be bought for my birthday party next week.

Paper hats — balloons — streamers — cakes — drinks — sweets

The items in the list have been separated with a dash instead of a comma.

1. Arrange these lists so that dashes separate the items in them.

   a) **Shopping list**
   1 kg sugar
   bottle of sauce
   250 g nuts
   2 pkts of potato chips
   1 carton of paper cups

   b) **Types of cars**
   Holden, Falcon, Toyota, Nissan, Volkswagen

2. Make a list of your favourite games and separate the items in the list with commas or dashes.
3. Make a list of your five favourite boys' or girls' names and separate them with commas.

Describing words — adjectives

Remember that an *adjective* is a word that describes. Look at this sentence.

The *feathertail* glider is a *tiny* marsupial member of the *possum* family.

The word 'feathertail' is an adjective because it tells what sort or type of glider.
The word 'tiny' is an adjective because it tells what sort of marsupial.
The word 'possum' is an adjective because it tells which family the glider belongs to.

1. Spot the adjective in these sentences.
   a) The little boy wandered along the bush trail looking at all the beautiful flowers.
   b) The noisy colourful parrots flew through the patch of dense bush.
2. Supply suitable adjectives that could be used to describe these things. Why are some adjectives more suitable than others?
   a) a desert
   b) a face
   c) a kitten
   d) a fire
   e) a thunderstorm

Replace the phrase

1. What other phrases could be used to replace the *italicised* phrase in this sentence? Make a list.
   The house *near the road* is old and haunted.
2. Supply other phrases to replace the *italicised* phrase in this sentence.
   The children ran to the park *across the bridge*.
3. Complete these sentences by adding a suitable phrase.
   a) The beautiful butterfly flew _____.
   b) The puppy, _____ belongs to me.
4. How many different phrases can you supply to complete this?
   a) Jack and Jill went _____ to fetch a pail of water.

CHECKPOINT 4
Action time

Write a short report
1. Prepare a short report about a native bird or animal that lives in an area near your home or school. The answers to these questions may help you in the preparation of your report.
   - Where does the animal or bird live?
   - What type of food does it eat?
   - Is it living in natural surroundings?
   - Do you think it is increasing or decreasing in number?
   - Does it have any natural enemies?
   - What can you do to help protect it?

Finish the story
1. a) Here is a story for you to complete. The first paragraph has been written for you. You will need to complete the story and give it a title.

   > Clarry the young feathertail glider was just over three months old. It was time for him to leave his mother's pouch for good. It was early evening as Clarry and his mother emerged from the nest and glided into a nearby tree. Clarry left his mother's pouch and ...

   b) Share your story with others in your class.

Write a letter

1. Write a letter to an animal park or zoo near your school or town and ask about their new attractions since your last visit. Your letter may start like this.

> The Manager
> Alton Animal Park
> Parkside 3487
> 13 May 1989
>
> Dear Sir/Madam
>
> I enjoyed my visits to your zoo two years ago. The animals I enjoyed the most were...

CHECKPOINT 5
Moving on

Task 1 Prepare an information chart
Prepare a chart on some other marsupial. Your chart should supply this information:
- A picture or drawing of the marsupial
- Where it can be found in the wild
- What it eats
- Natural enemies
- What is being done to protect it.

Task 2 Supply the missing information
Here is part of a chart that describes some of our native animals. Unfortunately the chart has been damaged. Can you make a chart like it and supply the missing information?

Name	Covering	Special features
kangaroo	fur	hops
koala		
wombat		
emu		
possum		

Task 3 Match the state and symbol
Each state and territory in Australia has an Australian animal as a symbol. Can you match the state or territory and its animal symbol?

Queensland, New South Wales, Victoria, Tasmania, South Australia, Western Australia, Northern Territory

numbat, Leadbeater's possum, hairy-nosed wombat, koala, platypus, Tasmanian devil, red kangaroo

UNIT 10
FOCUS   Letters

Read these two letters. The first letter is from a girl called Jane to her friend Alison. The second letter is from a friendly fuel pump called Fred to one of his customers.

From Jane to Alison

Dear Alison,

We've had a great holiday so far. We've been all over the Blue Mountains. Today we were at the Jenolan Caves. It's a great place. Uncle Greg and Aunty Yvonne came with us. We all went into one big cave called the Imperial Cave. It was a bit scary, especially when the lights went out. The limestone statues are really interesting. The guide was funny too. We are going to stay at the Cave House tonight. This is the best holiday I think I've ever had.

Love,
Jane.

The fuel pump complains

Dear Customer,

It's not often you get letters from petrol pumps but I'm fed up. You really must be more careful when you use me. Last week you yanked my rubber hose so hard I nearly fainted. If you pull gently I work just as well. Only yesterday your daughter crashed one of your car doors into my side. I almost cried with the pain. Please tell her to open the door slowly. And what about yesterday? You were in such a hurry you slammed down the handle of the hose so hard my chrome holders were sore for hours. Please treat me with care.

Your friendly fuel pump.
Fred.

CHECKPOINT 1
Discussion time

Comment and answer
1. Who were the writers in both the letters?
2. To whom were the letters addressed?
3. Why was the fuel pump complaining?
4. Which three complaints did the fuel pump make?
5. What if you were the fuel pump? Would there be any other complaints that you could think of?
6. What was the result when the customer pulled too hard on the rubber hose?
7. What was the result when Jenny crashed the door onto the pump?
8. Why do you think the fuel pump wrote the letter?
9. Could you describe the fuel pump's letter as a letter of complaint?
10. From which place was Jane's letter written?
11. Why did she write the letter?
12. Why do you think Jane included so much information about the Jenolan Caves?

CHECKPOINT 2
Exploring words

'Writing' words
1. Read the sentences below and use the 'writing' words to complete them.
    a) The _____ was written carefully at the top right hand corner of the page.
    b) She fixed the stamp onto the _____.
    c) The children wrote a letter to _____ information on the wool industry.
    d) The _____ was written at the bottom of the envelope.
    e) A letter of _____ about the traffic noise was written.
    f) At the bottom of the letter was the writers' _____.
    g) In the envelope was an _____ to the party.
    h) All the girls were _____ the letters they had written.

Writing words
signature
address
envelope
invitation
request
complaint
proofreading
postcode

'Same sound' words — homophones

> Here are some pairs of 'same sound' words. They sound the same but have different meanings.
>
> real — reel   blue — blew
> saw — sore   where — wear
>
> You remember! These pairs of words are called *homophones*.

1. Can you write the homophones of these words?
   a) break   d) for   g) hear   j) bare
   b) caught   e) steel   h) heal   k) whole
   c) write   f) road   i) type
   Can you write these words in sentences?

Word stems and families

> Look over these words.
>
> **sore**   **care**   **cave**
>
> The word stems 'ore', 'are', and 'ave' were used.

1. a) Add these beginnings to the word stem 'ore'.
      m,   ch,   sh,   sc,   st,   sp,   sw
   b) Now add these beginning letters to the word stem 'are'.
      m,   sh,   sn,   st,   sc,   gl,   fl
   c) Add these beginning letters to this word stem 'ave'.
      p,   kn,   st,   br,   sh,   sl,   beh

2. Let's build up some word families. The first one has been done for you.
   a) scare
      scare, scares, scared, scaring
   b) store
   c) glare
   d) share
   e) behave

3. Use some of the words you built in question 2 in these sentences.
   a) The goods were _____ on the shelves at the back of the shed.
   b) Were the children well _____ during the afternoon?
   c) The fierce lion _____ at the timid mouse.
   d) The girls began _____ out the sports gear among the six teams.

CHECKPOINT 3
Building blocks

Nouns, verbs and adjectives
1. Read over these sentences.

   All the family went into one huge cave.
   We saw some interesting limestone statues.

   a) In the sentences there are three nouns. What are they?
   b) There are two verbs. What are they?
   c) There are four adjectives. Identify these.

2. Select all the nouns in these sentences.
   a) On Monday the aircraft flew over the coast towards the island.
   b) The animal stumbled along the path.
   c) The boy on the oval could see the lights on the mountain.

3. Add nouns to these sentences.
   a) The _____ walked slowly to the _____.
   b) Many of the _____ came to the _____.
   c) My best _____ saw the _____ on the _____.

4. In these sentences the verbs have been left out. Which verbs can be used to complete the sentences? Where should they be placed?
   a) They up to the fence.
   b) My elder sister on the stage.
   c) A tall ship into the deep harbour.

Adjective/noun match up
1. Look over these two lists of words. The list on the left are adjectives, the list on the right, nouns. Can you match them?

hollow	knives
calm	weather
deep	log
sharp	tiger
loud	hole
fierce	noise

116

Capitals and full stops

1. Capital letters are needed when we set out letters.

> 7 Alaman Street
> Byron Bay 2481
> 6th April 1989
>
> Dear Joanne,
>
> Love from
> Chris

   a) Count the capitals used in setting out the above letter.
   b) Which words had capital letters?
   c) Capitals are used for days of the week. Make a list of other ways capitals were used in setting out this letter.

2. Capitals are needed on envelopes as well.

> Alison Carmody
> 37 Wagner Street
> Richmond
> Victoria 3121

   a) Look over the above envelope. Count the capitals.
   b) Make a list of the ways capitals were used on this envelope.
   c) Compare this envelope with others. Are there any other ways capitals are used on envelopes? You will probably find there are several other words that can be used instead of the word 'street'.

CHECKPOINT 4
Action time

Letter choices
1. Read this letter over. It has choices to be made at a number of points in the sentences. For those points where there is a set of alternatives choose which you consider is best. For those points where there are three blanks decide on three alternatives.

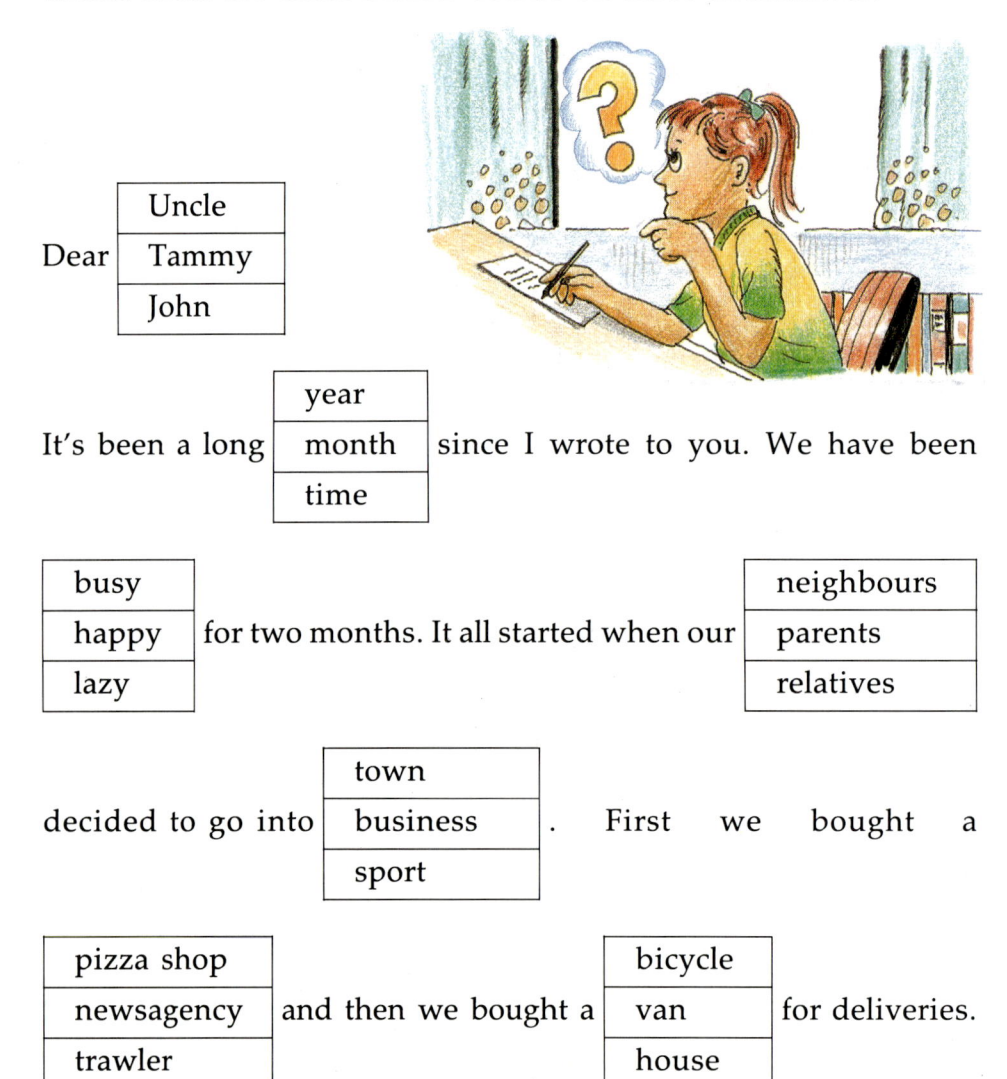

Dear | Uncle / Tammy / John

It's been a long | year / month / time | since I wrote to you. We have been

| busy / happy / lazy | for two months. It all started when our | neighbours / parents / relatives |

decided to go into | town / business / sport | . First we bought a

| pizza shop / newsagency / trawler | and then we bought a | bicycle / van / house | for deliveries.

118

There was lots of work to do. We had to clean up the ☐

and repair the ☐ . I often work on the ☐

while my sister does the ☐ .

                        Your friend,
                        Diane

Information seeking

Read this letter which is seeking information on a particular topic

> 137 Avalon Road
> Roseworthy SA 5371
> 3rd August 1989
>
> The Manager
> NSW Travel Centre
> 16 Spray Street
> Sydney NSW 2000
>
> Dear Sir/Madam,
> At school we are learning about the travel industry in some states of Australia. Would you be able to send a copy of booklets on New England and the Blue Mountains?
> I will use these booklets with booklets from other areas in our project work.
>
> Yours sincerely,
> Anna Carlos

Notice that this letter is quite short. It seeks information and therefore does not have to be a 'newsy' letter.

1. Write a letter. Write as if you need to find out about something for your class. Identify what information is needed. Decide to whom it should be written and check the address.

   Prepare a first draft of your letter. Share your writing with a partner. Ask him or her to read it. Then discuss the letter. Does the letter have any sentences that need changing in some way? Does it have things that need to be added or taken away?

   Check the spelling and check that all addresses and correct. Then address the envelope.

Mrs Helen Ryde
127 Alimah Crescent
SOUTH JOHNSTONE QLD 4854

Notice that there are no punctuation marks and that capitals are used for the entire last line.

Always include a return address on the back of the envelope.

Sender: Dianne Harris
27 Collins Avenue
RAYMOND TERRACE NSW 2324

Letters to authors

Dear Mr Whitaker,
I've just finished another of your great books. How did you ever think of Daleks? They must be the worst things in the universe. Please write some more books about them.
Your friend,
Craig Johns.

1. Have you a favourite book? Why not write a letter to its author? Share your writing with a partner after your first draft is finished.

CHECKPOINT 5
Moving on

Task 1   Letters to the stars
Do you have a favourite star, sports star, actor or television personality? Imagine you have been invited to meet this person but first you have to write telling about yourself and your interests. What would you write?

Task 2   Envelope enquiries
Read over the addresses on these envelopes. Discuss these points:
- Who would have written to these groups?
- Why would they write?
- What details might be in a letter to these groups?

Robbin's Bobcat Hire
103 Jacaranda Avenue
SWAN BEACH VIC 3903

Brismark Signs
53 Lagonda Street
ANNERLEY QLD 4103

TASK 3   Information display

Organise a class display. Your display could include three separate sections:

- a display of different kinds of letters, notes, cards and post-cards.
- a chart showing all the abbreviations that are used for these words:

    > street   road   avenue   parade   terrace
    > boulevard   corner   highway   crescent

- a chart showing the states and territories, and the range of post codes in these states and territories.
  For example:

    NSW and ACT 2000 to 2999

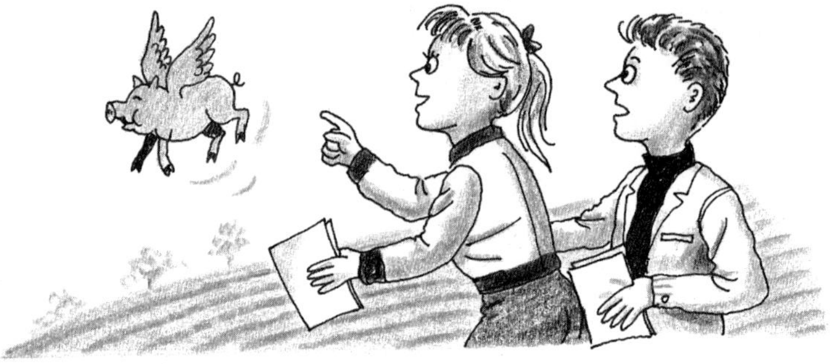

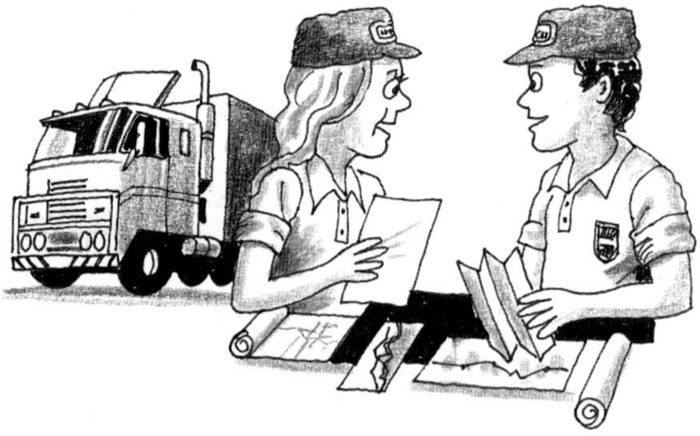

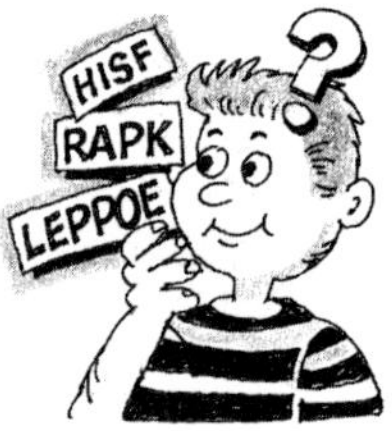
HISF
RAPK
LEPPOE

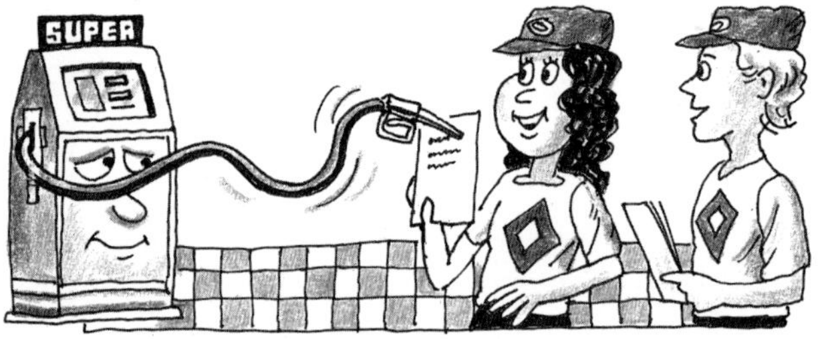
SUPER

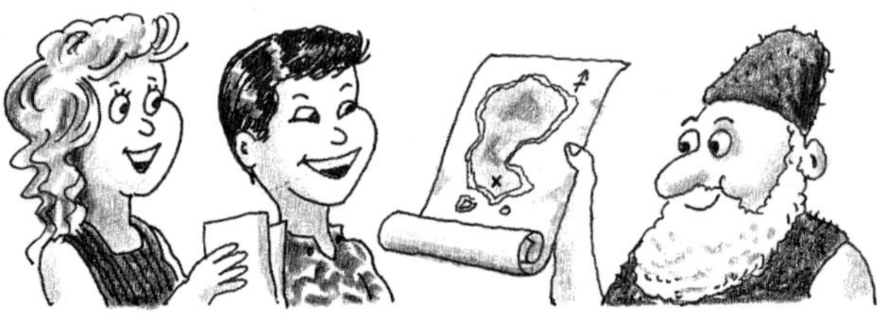

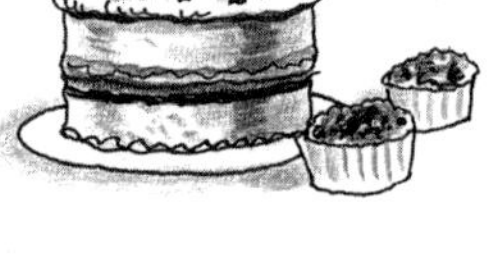

Teachers notes

Language checkpoints is a series of four books. Each book provides teachers at different levels in the primary school with a resource based on a 'whole language' approach to the teaching of language; an approach aimed at making the learning of language an interactive, meaningful process.

The four *Language checkpoints* books each contain a number of units. These units are linked together in such a way that the students experience coherent sequences of activities involving speaking, reading and listening. Each of the units presents stimulus material, both narrative and non-narrative, which students are invited to read and investigate. Each unit also includes a number of checkpoints. The checkpoints contain a wide range of language activities that relate to the units' stimulus material. The checkpoints also include short learning episodes that invite teacher expansion and encourage students to practise skills and processes. Each checkpoint becomes a platform on which the developmental activities in the following checkpoints are based.

It is not important that each child undertake to do every activity within a unit. In fact, it is important to encourage children to select those activities within a unit that are relevant to their levels of learning and ability, and their fields of interest. With careful teacher guidance, students can step from learning platform to learning platform, undertaking activities that promote feelings of success and enhance learning.

Language checkpoints incorporates and integrates the expressive modes of language; speaking and writing, with the receptive modes; listening, reading and observing. The format of the units facilitates this integration. They allow teachers to use classroom management strategies that emphasise students talking about what has been read and written, listening to authors reading what they have produced, and writing about what they have read and discussed.

	UNIT 1	UNIT 2	UNIT 3
FOCUS	**Literature** Extract from *The Sknuks* by Colin Theile	**Instructions** Making a glove puppet	**Verse** 'The Teams' by Henry Lawson 'Interstate Driver' by Ian Mudie
CHECKPOINT 1 Discussion time	• discussing opinions • predicting outcomes • identifying true/false statements • recalling details	• detecting differences • arranging in correct sequence • identifying true/false statements	• recalling details • discussing opinions • completing correct sequences
CHECKPOINT 2 Exploring words	• completing close exercise • using singular and plural forms • introducing the prefix	• using antonyms • identifying compound words • building words and word families	• using homophones • identifying and using contractions • building word families • identifying hyphenated words • preparing lists of rhyming words
CHECKPOINT 3 Building blocks	• introducing nouns • completing sentences • identifying direct speech	• introducing verbs • using verbs • locating capital letters and full stops	• introducing the subject and predicate of a sentence • locating capital letters and full stops in verse
CHECKPOINT 4 Action time	• introducing and using similes • introducing paragraphs • creating a story from an outline • completing a story from a beginning	• writing instructions for a picture sequence • changing from one form of instruction to another • composing sets of rules for games	• using rhyme in verse • composing syllable poems • writing acrostic poems
CHECKPOINT 5 Moving on	• letter writing • looking to the future • decoding messages	• preparing a puppet play • making a class display of instructions/directions • sketching and planning sets of instructions	• forming an acrostic poem display • writing descriptive verse • preparing lists of descriptive words

UNIT 4	UNIT 5	UNIT 6	UNIT 7
Recipes Chocolate fudge Fairy cakes Chocolate-chip cookies	**News report** 'A long road for Lloyd and an L-plate pup'	**Literature** Exract from *Pigs Might Fly* by Emily Rodda	**Diaries, logs and journals** Extract from *Robinson Crusoe* Extract from Bidu's journal
• discussing opinions • arranging in correct sequence • identifying cause-result relationships • identifying true/false statements	• recalling details • preparing questions • predicting outcomes	• recalling details • discussing opinions • identifying true/false statements	• identifying main ideas • arranging in correct sequence • discussing opinions
• identifying abbreviations • locating silent letters • using synonyms	• listening for synonyms • arranging in alphabetical order • cracking a number-letter code	• using singular and plural forms • building words and word families • introducing the suffix	• matching words and meanings • using antonyms • identifying and using compound words • identifying and using contractions
• identifying and using verbs • reviewing nouns • introducing the comma	• introducing proper nouns • identifying and using nouns and verbs • locating capital letters and full stops in a news report	• using sentence parts • identifying questions and answers • introducing quotation marks	• using nouns and verbs • adding phrases to expand sentences • using capital letters and full stops
• rewriting recipes in a different form • rearranging steps in correct sequence	• preparing a summary • writing a short report • writing a description • writing an imaginary short story	• completing a story from a beginning • using descriptive words • writing descriptive sentences	• preparing diary entries to match illustrations • expanding notes into complete sentences • writing of events happenings, thoughts and feelings
• making a class recipe book • making a recipe rack • classifying ingredients	• composing an autobiography • locating and collecting 'outback' stories	• reading and illustrating verse • investigating myths and legends • creating collages and mobiles	• composing a ficticious space journey log • locating and collecting diaries, logs and journals • detecting differences in various diaries.

	UNIT 8	UNIT 9	UNIT 10
FOCUS	**Advertisements** Cuddly Cat Jay's Joggers	**Article** 'The feathertail glider'	**Letters** The fuel pump complains Jane to Alison.
CHECKPOINT 1 Discussion time	• identifying true/false statements • recalling details • discussing opinions	• recalling details • identifying true/false statements • identifying main ideas • discussing opinions	• recalling details • identifying cause/result relationships • discussing opinions
CHECKPOINT 2 Exploring words	• preparing word lists • changing phrases to single words • arranging in alphabetical order	• using singular and plural forms • introducing the prefix and suffix • classifying word lists	• matching words and meanings • using homophones • building words and word families
CHECKPOINT 3 Building blocks	• introducing adjectives • matching nouns and adjectives • introducing adjectival phrases • using capital letters and full stops	• identifying and using adjectives • adding phrases to expand sentences • using commas	• Using nouns, verbs and adjectives • matching adjectives and nouns • using capital letters and full stops
CHECKPOINT 4 Action time	• preparing completed advertisements • preparing advertising posters • completing newspaper advertisements	• preparing a short report • completing a story from a beginning • writing letters	• choosing alternatives in letter writing • preparing a letter seeking information • writing a letter to an author
CHECKPOINT 5 Moving on	• making a collection of advertisements • collecting advertisements on tape • comparing commercials	• preparing an information chart • supplying missing information • matching State and symbol	• writing letters to stars • discussing letter contents • preparing and displaying charts